The (Almost) True Story
of a Man Called Jack

The (Almost) True Story of a Man Called Jack

I hope you enjoy 'Jack'

VIVIENNE LINGARD

Vivienne Lingard

Published 2020
by Artistry Publishing

ISBN 978-0-473-53398-4 (paperback)
ISBN 978-0-473-53440-0 (Epub)
ISBN 978-0-473-53441-7 (Kindle)

Printed by The Copy Press, Nelson, New Zealand.
www.copypress.co.nz

To the memory of my father, John Frederick Lingard Fowlds.

This story is written for my children, Lara, Duncan and Sarah, and for all the grandchildren who never knew his love.

I would like to thank my daughter Lara, who encouraged me to write about my father, my brother Bob (James) who put up with the many queries I sent him, and my sister Kath (Beverly), for agreeing to being a character in my family story. Sadly, my brother John (Colin) and my sister Marion (Maxine) died a few years before I began this story. I like to believe they would have enjoyed my version of events.

I also thank my husband Kerry for encouraging me to set deadlines. I may not have completed this manuscript without that sound advice. Also, thanks to Suzanne Hardy for her proofreading services, and Brian Pearce, who willingly searched the Upper Hutt archives for images.

Surely dreams are free

Jack stubbed his cigarette out in the gravel unsettling some dust, rubbed his dirtied shoe against his trouser cuff, slicked back his hair and re-tucked the pencil behind his ear. He had long set up the bookstall counter with boxes of sweets, and Racing Digests, ditched yesterday's papers in the bin for collection and popped a stack of fresh Dominions on the stand in front. The trains were running late. Couldn't moan; meant extra sales. Bored customers and all that. There were some daft buggers now; jumping off the platform and scooting over for the newspaper. He could usually persuade commuters to buy gum, or fizzy drink. Sweets sometimes. Maybe he could finish early; slope off after lunch, go grab some primer from Dulux. A couple of brushes. Oh, and a new scraper. Just one day of 'How's your missus' and a decent kip and she'd be his; well not exactly his, the boat was for the whole family to share. Not since he'd bought the truck, had he been this excited, like a bloody kid. Stupid bugger. But Jack trusted his instincts, and never had they seemed so right. The boat spelt good times, and boy, were they ever due some.

"What a day," Jack declared the next morning, pulling back the dull-brown curtain. Sparrows chattered and darted across his vision. His wife groaned. "C'mon my little darling," he said, plopping a kiss on her head. "Tommy's delivering her at eight." He tried another tack. "The kids are out there already, Kathleen."

"I'd never have guessed."

Jack left her with the sheets pulled over her head; at least she wouldn't see his disappointment.

What a ruckus! Four kids and only one delivered of a quiet temperament, though he couldn't blame God in this instance: the McPhee's had abandoned all religion well before the kids came along, but that's another story, better left for another day. Sophia held onto Bevvy's hand. "Here it comes, here it comes," the little one squealed. And here she comes alright. Jack hurried to the flattest part of the section, and helped guide Tommy's jeep so he'd miss the holes that Colin had dug 'for experiments, Dad' and hadn't yet filled in.

"Jeez, she's beautiful," Jack said, patting the hull once they'd unhitched the trailer, with the help of Tommy's boys. He was almost pleased that Colin had removed, and lost, the hinges to the old farm gate so that the boat could be eased through.

You could always bet on Bert Taylor snooping around; you heard the noise of him before you saw the man. And there he was buzzing to a stop, boot-heel against the front spokes, and wading through the knee-high grass, hat askew and carpenter's pencil stuck in the band, as usual.

"See you've fixed your brakes," Jack said.

"Like you've mown the grass."

"Snap."

Bert dropped the bike, losing it in the overgrown clover, adjusted the twine round his trousers and crouched, running his hand across the woodwork. "She's a beaut, Jack."

"She's that alright."

"Heavy though. But that's a Clinker for you."

"You know Tommy, don't you Bert?"

"You kidding? How's it going?"

"Better now," Tommy said, wiping a sleeve across his head. "And boys, you can go home if you want." Gary and Ron didn't hang around to argue. "Shame Moira's got jobs waiting," Tommy added.

"Shame alright," Jack said. He glanced up at the house, just a flicker of a curtain. A sign. Of what, he'd discover soon enough. Hoped it wasn't from God.

"Kids."

"Yes, Dad?"

"Got a job for you too."

To grin and bear

Kathleen hauled on the floral dress with ripped armholes and grumbled as she folded the bed base into the settee position; a daily ritual and even bigger chore. "I'm making a cuppa before sticking my head out there," she shouted at Jack. They had argued late into the night about the jolly boat and be damned if she was going to succumb to his charms, just yet. The French doors (what a misnomer) were flung open and she breathed in the scent of sweet peas she'd planted last spring. She glanced at the pile of fabrics on the treadle machine, sighed deeply, lifted the lid of the upright piano, bashed out the *Black and White Rag*, then left the living room (which doubled as their bedroom), strode the three and a half yards to the kitchen and boiled the jug, her black mood adjusting to the shape of the day. She put plates, spoons and a cereal box on the bench and ventured out the back door with a tray, mugs and a pot of tea, through the lean-to-cum-washhouse-cum-workshop. Everything doubled as something else in the McPhee household.

The dinghy lay in the long grass like a beached whale, white paint flaking, Jack and his mates cooing over it like lovesick teens.

"I thought dinghies were small conveyances," she said, placing the tea on the old concrete fountain, which no longer functioned – of course.

Jack knew to be concerned when Kathleen's voice dropped an octave and prepared his response as he supped on his tea.

That smile. "Yep, it is a little large – granted. But this is no ordinary dinghy. We've a Clinker-built boat here. All wood."

"I know you've come from Nordic stock, but isn't this taking it a bit far?" Kathleen nodded towards Tommy, and Bert, the silly old coot. Builder? Couldn't even fix his own bike.

Under Tommy's orders, Jack and Bert began positioning the bricks in strategic rows, on a slab of old concrete to the rear of the house, then lengths of 4"x2" were laid down. It took the three grown men, plus Colin and James giving their penny's worth, to carry the dinghy to its resting place. That didn't escape Kathleen's attention.

"Tea, boys? Breakfast, kids." She was about to call 'or you'll be getting it for lunch,' but let the words drop, as the children had clearly fallen in love with the idea of a dinghy and had joined in the venture with more enthusiasm than a trip to the pictures could muster.

She smiled, despite her misgivings, and wondered when the children would figure out that they lived thirty miles from the sea and that the truck wasn't rigged with a tow bar.

Undercurrents

Jack needed more time to finish off the last of the sanding. He calculated a week after that for the paint job, and that should do it. He stood back from the boat and adjusted his cap. Sweat glued his hair to his forehead in a flat band. The school holidays were halfway through, which left three more weeks of labour. Yep, the kids would get to see it afloat. And Kathleen. He chuckled, as he'd not told her about the boathouse Tommy had rented out at Titahi Bay. Kathleen had had a go at him that very morning, how he'd end up letting the lot of them down – again. She'd flung a leg out of the blankets, left it dangling, hoisted the other alongside it and pulled herself into a sitting position. The black cloud hung heavy on her shoulders today, that's for real. "Wish we could get a proper bed," she'd grumbled. There was a list, there often was, mostly about money and time-wasting pursuits that only one of them might benefit from or enjoy. He knew he'd let her down, on the rare occasion. But this time he knew he'd got the formula right. Tommy was in the middle of negotiating a new home for him and his brood, far from Silverstream, but near the bay – lucky bugger. He would take care of the boat. Full stop. Jack knew only too well that his own house needed work, or, pulling down entirely. Didn't she think he also hated the way the yellowing paint had crazed, and the windows had warped, so that few would open anymore? But the boat would give them a reason to drive to the beach, catch fish and enjoy the bloody holidays for a change. Yes, indeedy! Happiness is what that boat would bring.

"Jack. Lunch?" Kathleen was standing in the doorway, balancing Bev on a hip.

"You'll do your back in with that tub of a kid." he said. His wife grinned and dipped her dark head to kiss the top of Bev's fair one.

Ah, Kathleen; bright as a button, too smart for him if the truth be known, but past pupils had benefitted from that quick-fire brain, as much as their own kids did. Shame her drunken old bat of a mother caused her to quit university and lose the scholarship she'd been given. She could have been a professor; imagine that – gaining a PhD. She might have been known as Doctor Kathleen McPhee, rather than, 'the wife of that Jack with the travelling library'.

There she was, the old Chrysler, parked up on the street, reminding him it was time to be behind the wheel again. Good old girl. Proud of her he was, with his very own brushstrokes spread along her flanks: *The Gloucester Travelling Library* – in black paint. The guilt was piling up as he'd also neglected the book stall, though not to the same degree; setting off at six a.m. to the yards as always, but knocking off by ten a.m. or earlier if possible to get back to the boat. Naturally his dear wife had noticed; she had eyes in the back of her head that one. And hearing? Sharp as a tack. Jack headed to the washhouse, hooked his thumbs in his overall straps, and dropped them to his feet.

Jack and the Travelling Library

He ducked his head into the kids' room, where they sat around the only table in the house. "Two, Four, Six, Eight, you lot are bogging in all right."

"We're going swimming at the river, Dad. Mum said."

"Did she now?"

Kathleen stepped out from the kitchen opposite. "Yes, I did Jack McPhee. And I said that you were coming with us."

"But Kathleen – I'm almost done."

"And that goes for me too. Four children with one parent as far as I can see."

"Please come, Daddy, please, please, please." He'd have to go. Bugger.

"Lunch, Jack."

He scraped out a stool and sat beside Kathleen at the fold-down kitchen bench, where he could see into the kids' room if he leaned back, which he did, raised his right thumb to his nose and wriggled his fingers. They giggled back. "Go grab your togs." Kathleen called, "And roll them up in the towels like I showed you. Finish your lunch, James. You too, Bevvy. But we're not leaving until one of you feeds that jolly rabbit."

"Yes, Mum."

"Now, Jack."

"Kathleen."

"I really wish you hadn't got that boat."

"Would you like me to set fire to it?"

"Can't you ever be serious?" She pushed up from her seat. Jack pulled her skirt. "You have to trust me on this."

"It's just that ... oh forget it. You just don't get it, do you?" He pulled her to him, kissed those stubborn lips. And again, until she slapped at his arm. "The kids, Jack." And there they were in the hallway.

"Well, they have to learn about the bees and birds sooner or later," he said. Kathleen grabbed a tea towel from the sink and flicked it at him. "Not from me," she said, "not from me."

"Get those bums in the truck," he told the children, "before your mother hurts me."

*

Jack stood in the shallows, pants rolled up, watching his white feet rippling under the water. He knotted his handkerchief corners and shoved it on his head. It was bloody hot. Good old Kathleen, swimming with the kids, doing that old-fashioned side-stroke. He began singing, knowing he was within earshot of his wife. She liked him singing, and she liked this one... *Light she was and like a fairy, and her shoes were number nine ... herring boxes ...Oh my darling, Clementine.* He stopped, remembering the heroine drowned. He remembered too, how he'd once loved swimming. Pushing through the sea, jumping for the breakers and riding the waves to shore. Sister Ignatius from the orphanage would be waiting, clapping wildly, her long black skirts brushing the damp sand. Back then the psoriasis was a mere patch but now it smothered his legs with ruddy lumps and flaking skin. No togs for Jackie boy these days. Sister told him it was hereditary; but how would he know? His mother died soon after his brother Henry was born, and he knew stuff all about his father. There were rumours: that he'd gone bush; whaling; been sighted in Bluff; Invercargill and Stewart Island. If he managed to track the bugger down, he'd force him to roll up his trousers.

Scaly shins or not, he could see himself helping Tommy push the dinghy out from the beach, leaping in, grabbing the oars and the pair of them laughing like a couple of loons. And hadn't Sister always insisted, that salt water was good for his skin?

What was that? A kid thrashing the water, his head bobbing. Without thinking Jack hot-stepped it along the stones, unbuckling his belt. He kicked his trousers aside and he was in the river, and diving under. Shit. His ears were hurting. But he had him. Up to the surface and on his back, he kicked out for the bank, stones scraping his arse when he hit the shallows.

He flopped on his side, lungs pounding. The rescued kid coughed hard a few times then raced off, screaming. Jack sat hugging his knees, hair flopping forward, wondering how far his walk of shame in his undies might be. "Here." A woman, tears streaming, held out a towel to him. He stood, turned his back and tied it around his hips. "You saved my boy," she said, and hugged him. The shivering boy, clung to his mother's skirt, a towel enveloping his skinny shoulders.

More shouting. Colin and James heading his way, waving the khaki trousers. Nothing like advertising the fact, he thought. "Could I have your phone number?" the woman asked. "I'd like to thank you properly. A cup of tea? Lunch maybe?"

"I've two more of these," he said, hooking a thumb towards his boys.

"It'll be my pleasure ..."

"Jack."

"Sylvia."

"The number's 5041."

With his pants reclaimed, Jack looked to where the grass met the stones and where the woman was packing up her things. She looked up. Waved. He took in her red spotted sundress and the smile.

Kathleen was sitting in the truck, arms folded, looking like she'd sucked a lemon. Jack bundled the boys in the back where they sprawled out on the mattress, which filled in the gap between the books held in by wires on shelving both sides. Colin crawled up the front and tapped his mother's shoulder. "You should have seen Dad."

Jack put a finger to his lips, refrained from saying 'shut up.' "Dad saved a boy," James said.

Kathleen was embarrassed that he'd been seen in his undies he supposed, but what he never expected, was the cold shoulder treatment the whole way home, and then the barrage about how their children might have lost a father, never mind her losing a husband when they reached the other end.

Never mind that he'd saved the kid.

The pickup

Jack was so annoyed with Kathleen's behaviour down the river, that he chose not to inform her of the dinghy's next adventure and worked like two men to get the boat finished by the week's end. He bribed the children to make excuses why they couldn't go out Saturday, if their mother should ask, and promised extra sweets from the bookstall come Sunday. Jack always gave each child a small white bag filled with jelly beans, Minties or a chocolate fish, which they munched on while listening to the children's radio programme. Gave him and Kathleen time for a bit of nookie, if he was lucky. So far, so good. Tommy would be here early. Good old Tommy, he'd miss him being so far away. What a lucky guy – being able to walk through lupin-clad dunes to the sea. But what was he thinking? Now they'd both have weekend jaunts to the beach like he'd dreamed of.

He dipped his brush in the blue paint and began picking out the rim, when Bert rode up the grass. "Lookin' good, Jack," he said, legs astride the crossbar. "Can't say the same for the house."

Jack clenched a fist. Sometimes, Bert Taylor ... "Yeah, I know. On my list Bert. On my list."

"Give us a call when yer ready to move the boat," the old fellow said, and rang his rusted bike bell. Brakes not fixed, of course.

Jack slipped out of bed at sparrows' fart two days later, and although he tip-toed along the hall, the kids heard him and sneaked out from their room. Jack held a finger to his lips. "You better jump in with Mum," he whispered to Bev. "Keep quiet," he hissed at the rest of them and thankfully they obliged. Even if Kathleen poked her nose out the window, she wouldn't see much in this light.

Colin and James grabbed an oar each, faced each other, pretending they were warriors. Sophia was trying to 'shush' them. "Shit." James had dropped his oar. And there was Tommy backing in the trailer. Old Bert turned up as promised, so as before, except in reverse, they hoisted up the dinghy and carried it down the grass and laid it against the bandaged supports on the trailer. Jack held onto his knees for a minute, regaining his breath.

"Too many beers I reckon," Bert said, thumping his back.

"Speak for yourself, you old bugger."

"Dad!"

"It's his name," he told Sophia, and set his mates laughing.

Ten minutes later, the dinghy was loaded and packed up tight like a sausage for the run to the sea. "Take it slow, Tommy, won't you?"

He laughed. "See you and the rest of the company later, eh?" Jack could only hope for the best. The sky was still pink, blushed as a baby's bottom. It would work out. It had to.

Jack gathered the three children around him. "I want you all to head back to bed for a bit. Read, if you can't sleep. I need to talk with your mother that's all, before we head to the beach."

Kathleen had been slaving away on the family sewing all

week, which hadn't helped to shift the black cloud from her shoulders, though he'd thought up a wee scheme to forestall the storm. Time to put plans in action. He crept into the kitchen and recovered the extra loaves he bought the previous day and began slicing them. He hadn't got far when Sophia joined him and without speaking began to butter the bread. He patted her hand and kept slicing. Jack spread Marmite on half the loaf and Sophia put peanut butter on the rest. A special one with honey for little Bev. The cheese, tomatoes and apples he'd get from the food safe on the way out. Buy drinks when they got there. Fizzy. The kids loved it.

He and Sophia filled the wicker hamper, folded tea towels on top. Added three extra mugs. "Back to bed, lovey," he said to his daughter, and proceeded to make tea for her mum. Plan B. With the one and only tray laid with an embroidered cloth, teapot, toast and jam, he walked the few paces into the lounge. He set the breakfast on the small round table and climbed back into bed, gently rolling Bevvy aside. Kathleen was awake, he always knew by the change in her breathing. He leaned over and kissed her hair.

"Thought you might like a cuppa." She pulled herself to a sitting position. He followed suit.

"Toast too?"

"Nothing's too good for my darling." He offered his bristled cheek and she kissed it, glancing toward the sleeping child.

"You're up to something," she said.

"All I'll say, is that I want to you in the frock you made last week when you arise, m'lady. And a touch of lipstick for those lovely lips."

"Jack ..."

"I'll be off now. Got things to do."

"People to see?"

"Just trust me. Okay?"

The launch

Kathleen clambered into the truck, clutching her sunhat, which Jack insisted she bring along. She did wonder why he'd parked further up the street and exited through the front door, which no-one generally used. Perhaps they were off to Eastbourne? She and Jack played tennis there before they married. She'd been good at that; like so many other things.

She was exhausted, and tried not to nod off, knowing how her husband hated that. School was back the following week and she had to admit she was thankful. Once Bev was at school, she was determined to return to teaching; it wasn't only for the money, though they certainly needed it. She had liked teaching a good deal and liked nothing better than instruction in some of her favourite subjects; arithmetic, writing and English, to name a few. But what she enjoyed most was the piano, which she opened classes with each morning. And singing; she might have been a professional singer. If only. If only her father hadn't been killed in the Great War and left her alone with her mother. The 'broken widow' as Kathleen sometimes thought her. Helpless and desperately needy. She wouldn't examine the reasons she had married Jack too closely. What if she had simply been swayed by a uniform; as shallow as the girls who dated the American GI's in the war. She had never forgotten how her mother raved about the 'strumpets' flooding Wellington's streets, clinging on the soldiers' arms.

Warm fingers clamped her hand. She woke with a start. Looked about. Checked the children in the back. All but Colin were asleep. Peculiar to say the least. That wasn't Wellington Harbour outside the window. Manuka dotted the hills; cowered by prevailing winds.

"Where are we, Jack?"

"Porirua coming up. Titahi Bay shortly after."

"Oh."

"Thought a picnic might be nice."

"What picnic?"

"The one Sophia and I put together."

Sophia looped her arms over the seat. Grinned at her mother. "We've got to get drinks, that's all."

It wasn't often she was lost for words, but nothing came to mind.

"We're having fizz," the boys said. "And maybe ice cream if we're good."

Kathleen knew better than to challenge that one, but imagined the probable results on the journey home.

"Everyone out," Jack called, pulling in to an asphalt parking area. Ripples of heat rose from the truck's bonnet. "Hats on, the lot of you. And don't forget your togs." He climbed into the back once they were out and claimed the picnic hamper.

A track led through the dunes. Sophia pulled at a rogue foxglove, gathering a handful of flowers in her palm. "You put them on your fingers Bev. Like this." Where did she learn that? her mother wondered. The sand led onto a concrete path leading towards a short row of brightly painted boat sheds. The wooden doors were open on the blue one, second in. A man with a mop of blonde hair stepped out on the ramp. Tommy.

"Morning, Kathleen."

Kathleen looked at Jack. He grinned. Boy, was she astonished? "G'day, mate."

"G'day yourself, Jack."

"Mum. Mum. Come see the dinghy." She joined the boys on the ramp and stood, arms akimbo, scrutinising the boat which had sat in their yard, its trim picked out in blue. Tommy and Jack giggled like a couple of five-year-olds. This was a setup. Her mind tracked back to the early morning, the leaving via the front door …

"You going to help us get her down there?" Tommy asked the boys. They threw their arms up shaking them flat out, like children did in class.

"Me."

"Me."

Jack was at her shoulder, put an arm around her and squeezed. "What do you make of her, Kathleen?"

"I'll save my verdict, once I've seen it float," she said. There was no need to say any more.

Jack removed his arm. "Come on then, help us shove it out."

Kathleen joined Colin at the back of the dinghy; Tommy and Jack pulled from the prow, Sophia and James along the sides and Bev, like smartypants herself, rode pride of place on a small bench up the front.

Jack at Trentham Camp

Jack lifted Bev down as they neared the water. "Stay near Mum," he said, rolling his trousers to his knees. "This is men's work."

Colin and James were up to their waists already, holding the boat when Tommy yelled, "In you go, Jack." He clambered over the side. The boat rocked sideways and righted itself as Jack gained his balance. "Sit down, or she'll tip." And then the pair of them were in. Kathleen stood on the strip of wet sand, dreading that the boat would turn over. She held up an arm to shield the glare from the sea. An oar slipped. The boat lifted. She held her breath.

"I'll get it, Dad," James yelled, jumping clear when Tommy gripped both oars and pushed out to deeper water. Jack grabbed his hat and waved it high. Kathleen lifted her hand.

The waves rolled in gently splashing her calves with sun-warmed water. The boys were swimming now, practising the crawl she'd shown them at the beginning of summer. Sophia sat back from the sea, burying her sister's legs with sand and Bev loving every minute of it. Kathleen spread out a large striped towel and sat beside the girls, knees drawn up, her arms around her shins, wishing she could share the family's happiness.

It was Jack's cavalier ways which had attracted her at first, a tonic to her tamped down existence. She blamed her mother, for her past misery and the situation Jack found her in: a spinster, looking after a sick woman. Kathleen shuddered; hating herself for still having that dragged down feeling, even though her mother was no longer around.

The boat was coming in; the men ecstatic after the maiden voyage. "It's watertight," Jack shouted.

"Bet you're pleased about that, Kathleen?" said Tommy,

releasing the oars as the dinghy reached the shallows. Colin and James clambered in once the boat was anchored, sitting on the seat, enjoying the slight rock of the waves.

"Can we come out next time, Uncle Tommy?"

"Dad?"

"We want to go fishing."

"Will next week be too soon?" Tommy said. "Thought I'd bring my lot out too."

Kathleen didn't mind his children, but nine altogether in one boat (minus lifejackets), was a disaster in the making. Tommy attached a long pole through the anchor and led them back to the boat-shed barefoot, his feet caked with sand.

"I'm all itchy," Bev said. "The sand's up my bum." Kathleen raised her eyebrows at Jack, took hold of the girl's hand and marched her along to the changing sheds, stripped her down and made her bend over under a running cold tap. She reached in the string bag for clean bloomers and pedal-pushers and stuffed a very disgruntled daughter into them.

"Can't have been pleasant," Tommy said when they returned, his face creasing into a grin. "We heard her from here."

"It was VERY, VERY cold," said Bev.

"Will this make it better?" And the sour look changed to smiles when he handed her some fizz.

"You seem well set up," she said, when Tommy reached into a storage bin and handed creaming soda and a straw around. "I've been coming out here for a while," he said, "since taking her over." Her thoughts were of Moira, at home with five kids.

"Been getting the boathouse ready for the dingy," Jack added. As if that let him off the hook.

Jack dozed off after lunch, his straw hat over his face like a farmer. Bev was asleep, snuggled into his side, Sophia was scribbling in a sketchbook and Colin had his head in a *Popular Mechanics* magazine.

"Would you like a wee go in the boat, Kathleen?" Tommy asked. "I'll keep it anchored if you like?" he said, when he saw her mouth had dipped down.

James dropped the stick he was feigning hits with. "I'll help you, Mum," he said.

"I'd like that," she said. And this time, she removed her sandals, to walk down the beach.

There's always a first time for everything

Being free of the house gave her spirits a lift, if only for the short time away from the crumbling mansion. At the corner she tipped Timmy the tabby from the wicker basket onto the Robertson's brick wall, rubbing his head on release. She hooked the basket on her left elbow and reached for Bev's hand. The boys were ahead, feigning tolerance with the other's existence. No surprise there. Colin was getting a bit pudgy, she thought, but that's what happened if one shied exercise. James was like a pea on a drum, endlessly moving around. Sports mad he was; cricket, tennis, rugby, anything with a ball. Today she'd lent him her old racquet, as he had told her, 'I have to have one, Mum.' She hoped he'd excel at sport as she'd once done.

"What is it, Sophia?" She'd stopped, clapped her hands to her ears. "Come on, it's only a train."

Kathleen at tennis

"I hate the whistle."

Kathleen laughed, "Don't be so silly."

The girl was soft, goodness knows why.

The children crossed the road at the corner and she watched until they dropped Sophia at the gate to the Infant classrooms. Instant chaos; Colin chucking James's schoolbag along the footpath. "Stop it," she yelled. And now James was hitting his brother. She refrained from running after them and giving them a clip each around the ear. That'd wait till they got home.

Bev tugged her hand. "Watch me. Watch me."

"What?"

"I can stand on one leg without wobbling."

"I can see that. Now, do you remember what I told you about crossing the road?"

"Of course. Look left, right, left and cross."

Bev stomped onto the narrow bridge beside the rail tracks.

"And here?"

"I didn't forgot."

"Forget."

Kathleen grabbed her hand, checked the tracks and crossed. She wouldn't have bothered with the Four Square on the main road, if she hadn't run out of Blue bags for the copper. Washing days were anathema to her, though she did recognise a mild enjoyment when watching the blue seep through the clear water, then pegging out the sheets. She'd raise the grooved wooden prop in the middle of the line, and watch the white and spotless sheets billow, knowing the entire street could see.

She glanced over to the corner section opposite theirs. Mrs

'Crumbling Mansion'

Reagan's line was empty. Let's see what she does when the whites go out? Jack didn't believe her, but the woman would have the same item hanging on her line within the hour. Nuts. Quite nuts, she thought, dragging through the long grass of her own section, when her foot sank in one of Colin's holes; a thick sludge of muddy water at the bottom. Unconcerned, Bev had grabbed the tyre which hung from the scrappy apple tree and swung it out over the bank, missing her mother's head by inches.

Kathleen sat on the back steps, easing off the sodden shoe with the heel of the other. There was a brief moment when she might have wept, if she hadn't seen the scythe propped against the redundant fountain.

"Go inside, and stay there," she bellowed at her daughter. "There's something I have to do."

23

Rocking a different boat

The early mornings were a drag now the kids were back at school; the family barely awake when Jack crept from bed, had a rough shave, threw the 'uniform' of baggies and braces over yesterday's shirt, and headed under bleary skies to Naenae railway yards. The newspapers were always waiting in fat bound-up piles, and he'd lug them into the renovated army hut, slash the binding and heap them up on the fold-down counter.

A dash outside with the wire stands, exchanging the old advertising for new, and the commuters would be queuing, grabbing for the Dominion Post and a packet of fags, as soon as they got to the front.

He loved the chat; the 'howdy-do's'. But lately something was missing. It couldn't be age; he wasn't yet thirty-eight; whatever it was that he couldn't name precisely, was nibbling his insides away. He'd have a catch-up with Joe Wong before setting off home; the man was always good for a laugh.

Joe was packing up his fruit truck, ready to take to the streets. Towards the gorse-covered hills was Joe's soon-to-be-his new shop.

"You want I take you now, Jack." he said, for the second time in the conversation.

"I've got to get back …"

He laughed. "Follow me. Won't take long."

They pulled up opposite a block of three shops: a dairy, a bookshop renewing its lease and Joe's soon to be green-grocer's shop. They both climbed out and leaned on the tray of his truck. "Mr Williamson is nice guy, Jack. He talk good business, like me."

Naenae bookstall.

"I am interested, don't get me wrong. But it's..."

"Mrs Kathleen perhaps?"

"Not quite."

"It money?"

Jack nodded.

"I have. You not. Always can find a way." Joe shook Jack's hand. "And anyway, lease not up until next year." Off he went, expelling diesel fumes with every gear change. Jack coughed and climbed into his Chrysler, did a U-turn, and stopped outside the bookshop, thinking he might bring Kathleen down; see what she thought of leasing. He pulled the throttle, turned the key, and drove back up the Eastern Hutt Road, which was undergoing major changes. Where rimu and cabbage trees once filled the valley, crops of state houses had replaced them, sprouting up from Petone through to Taita along the eastern side of the river. It wouldn't be long before the temporary camps he visited were mowed down as well; though that may have its advantages, given his recent thinking. Kathleen seemed to have come around to the dinghy's benefits so well, that he thought she deserved a treat. Flowers. That's the ticket.

"Won the Art Union, have we Jack?" Mr Narayan asked, wrapping newsprint around the stems of six red roses.

"I just might have," he said, and went off whistling.

The whistle dried on his lips when he saw the results of Kathleen's labours. He parked up, walked through the hacked grass, discovering bricks in the hole in the ground he'd meant to have Colin fill in. The scythe was resting where he'd inadvertently left it; an innocent player in the family warfare. He moved quietly through the house and got as far as the children's room, where Kathleen was asleep on Sophia's bed, her arm around little Bev. He retreated, filled an empty milk bottle with water, stuffed the roses in and walked out the way he'd come.

James and Colin found him on the same step their mother had sat on and chewed over her troubles earlier that day, his head bowed, sweat pouring from him. "Take it easy with your mother," he said to James. And to Colin, "If you ever dig one of those damned holes again..."

"What, Dad?"

"I'll stick your head in one."

The boy began sobbing. "It was an experiment," he snuffled. "I was measuring which hole filled fastest with rainwater."

"Here; blow your nose." And Jack handed him a large handkerchief. "I would never have done it. Sorry, son."

Kathleen chose not to speak all evening, except to the children when dishing out meals. Come bedtime she came into the living room, where he'd already opened the settee and sat reading a mystery pinched from his own library, in a nearby armchair. "There's only room for one of us in here tonight," she announced, pulled open the bedcovers and climbed in. "And turn the light off when you're finished."

Some might have called him yellow, but Jack well knew how to gauge the temperature. He slumped off to the kids' room, humped the spare mattress from behind the door, grabbed a torch from the lean-to and headed to his truck.

Swings, roundabouts and rollercoasters

Jack woke, feeling like shit, and he sure as hell didn't feel like the library run. The door squeaked as he shoved in with the mattress and dumped it in the hall. Silence. At least he'd be first in the bathroom for a change. A lick and a promise, was all he was good for, never mind yesterday's clothes.

The motor was cold and he was about to haul on the choke when Sophia knocked on the passenger's window. "I want to come with you."

"Up you get then," he said, reaching for her hand and pulling her in. "Mum not need you this morning?" Sophia didn't reply, and when he looked over, she was sniffing back tears.

"I'm pleased you want to join your old dad."

"You're not old."

"Thanks," he said. "You can be my helper."

He headed over Silverstream bridge and up the main road to Upper Hutt. The truck drubbed on the road, the knot holes in the floorboards enriching the sound. It was oddly comforting. He pulled in at the bakery, taking Sophia with him. She stuck her nose close to the glass cover, where lamington slices, and butterfly cakes were on show. "Choose one, Sophia." She pointed to the butterfly cakes.

"One of those and a fly cemetery," he said. The hair-netted woman screwed up her face. "Oh sorry, I meant fruit mince slice."

"You always say that, Dad."

"It gets them every time, Sophia," he laughed. "Every time." For now, he was happy, with his daughter beside him, and the freedom the travelling library could bring. He finished his fly cemetery, engaged the gears and glanced at Sophia, licking cream off her fingers.

"How much is that doggie in the window?" He sang.

"Wait, Dad." Sophia swallowed, and answered, *"The one with the wag g i ly tail."*

"How much is the doggie in the window?"

"I do hope that doggie's for sale."

"What do you want, Sophia?"

"I don't want a bunny or a kitty."

"I don't want a parrot that talks. So, what do we want, Sophia?"

"A DOG WITH A WAG G I LY TAIL!"

"You have cheered me up no end," he said, turning off the main road and into Mangaroa. A few farmer's wives trotted out with their books after he'd parked up and tooted. The usual suspects;

Mrs Morris with her neighbour, Mrs Gordon, returns in their bags, gossiping. Dear old ducks; wanting romance or detective stories, though neither had a particular preference.

He put the latest Ngaio Marsh and Agatha Christie's to the front of the shelf. Nothing much new in the Romance section; he could guarantee that. Sophia chalked up the sale items on the small blackboard, as her father directed.

"You've a clever one there," Mrs Gordon told him. "She has lovely printing for one so young."

"And that she does, Mrs Gordon, that she does," Jack said, giving Sophia a hug.

"Where next, Dad?"

"To my old stamping ground."

It was always somewhat odd hawking his wares in the old Trentham Camp, where he'd hung out with his army mates not so very many years before. He counted on his fingers. It was getting on for nine; how did that happen so fast? He still saw Dave Vickers, who was groundsman these days at the bowling club. They'd both been in charge of stores, no overseas malarkey for either of them. Flat feet had kept them grounded, a fact he kept under his hat. He wound down his window, stuck two fingers in his mouth and belted out a whistle; his signature one for Dave.

"G'day, Jack," Dave bellowed back from the centre of the green. "Grab a beer sometime?"

"Gotcha." He continued around the block and pulled in beside a row of prefab houses, old army stock, slowly filling with civilians. Cheap without the cheerful, he thought, as he opened up the back doors of the truck and lowered down the steps. His place might not be much, but at least it was his – if you didn't count the twenty-five-year mortgage.

Mr and Mrs Collins were approaching; he a telephone pole of a man, plus hat, and she the prize pumpkin, complete with rosette. Sophia piped up: *"Jack Sprat could eat no fat, his wife could eat no lean..."* Jack stood gently on his daughter's foot and squashed the rhyme nicely.

"Nice to see you both," he said, ushering the husband in ahead of him and was about to reach for Mrs Collin's elbow, when he noticed a young woman in red headscarf and sunglasses, some yards off. He helped Mrs Collins up the steps, snapped open a folding chair for her husband, and stepped back onto the street, suggesting Sophia keep quiet for the time being.

The scarf-wearing woman came alongside, removed her glasses, looked at the truck, then Jack. "It *is* you."

"Sylvia?"

Jack and his army mates

"My apologies for not phoning. My friend …" She looked behind her. "Pam took us to the river that day."

Jack shuffled his feet. "How is the youngster?" he said, suddenly unsure of himself.

"Better. Oh, Jack, this is Pam; we're off to the Camp pictures."

"Gene Kelly. Lucky you."

Sophia tugged at his trouser leg. "Dad."

Sylvia smiled. "Look, why don't you bring your family around next Sunday."

Jack muttered something like 'I think I said I'd play tennis', desperately searching for an excuse.

"Do you know my father, Mr Atkins, the piano teacher?"

"Yep. Blue Mountain Road."

"That's where I am." Jack watched them walk away, when Sylvia turned back. "I forgot to say; after morning church." He waved, wondering how on earth he'd win Kathleen around.

More regulars. "Got your magazines in, Betty. And Arthur, the Graham Greene novel you were after," he said.

Jack waited for the Collins' to vacate the truck before ushering Betty and Arthur in. "Take your time," he said, handing over *The end of the affair.* He went to the doorway and rolled a cigarette from his Park Drive tin and puffed away until he spotted more customers. He rubbed the butt out with a heel.

"Dad," Sophia said, when they were on the road again. "Can I talk now?"

"You can sing if you want," he laughed.

"*Old MacDonald?*"

"*With a Honk Honk here and a Honk Honk there …*" Jack punched the horn for effect as they went through the verses, getting louder with each one. The day was working out pretty well, whichever way he looked at it, and he wasn't about to sneeze at that.

A touch of genius

He pulled up at the gate, or rather, the square concrete posts where a gate had once hung. Jack and Sophia trod down the four steps, across the patched concrete of their front yard and stopped. Colin had appeared from the back of the house waving a broom handle; a white singlet tied to its end, the limp cotton flapping.

"Battle over is it, son?"

"Ask Mum." Jack put a finger to his lips. Kathleen was at the piano – Handel. He used to sing this all the time. He stepped inside the French doors. *"Where'er you walk..."* He shuffled through tenor, found baritone – *"...cool gales shall fan the glade. Where'er you sit - shall crowd into a shade..."*

His wife turned to him; her regal profile illuminated. She was wearing the newly-made frock and a smidgeon of lipstick. "I'm sorry, Jack," she said. "I shouldn't have made such a fuss. I really don't know what gets into me, I really don't. And the flowers, that was such a nice..."

"Come here," he said, pulling her to him, hugging her tight.

Colin sidled past his parents, Sophia following him. He sat on the piano stool and continued the melody his mother had been playing, a little fast, a few missed notes, but it was unmistakably *Where'er You Walk.*

"How did you learn to do that?" Jack said.

"I listened to you singing when Mum played."

"Fancy that."

"And I just practised it. Like an experiment." Colin was flushed and anxious.

"How about you accompany me, Colin?"

"Really?"

"Yes really, my little genius. Now, let's take it from the top."

On the loose

Colin closed the piano lid. "Do you want to see what Mum and I did, Dad?" He led Jack to the apple tree. "See. We raked up the grass. Mum said it'd be good for compost."

It looked better with the holes, he thought.

"She wants a vegetable garden."

Is that so, Kathleen. Jack surveyed the mess of spindly bush where weeds ran amok.

"What are you doing?"

"Colin and I are planning a garden." Sophia plucked a rosehip from the dying bush. "I can help."

He laughed. "Thanks for the offer."

"Daddy."

"Bev." He scooped her up, twirled her around, and dropped her gently at Kathleen's feet.

Jack turned to his son. "Thanks, for helping your mother," he said, "Now that deserves treat." The boy's eyes widened.

"Yep. We'll be off to the beach again tomorrow."

"Really."

Jack and girls in original 'garden'

"Only if Whiffy turns up – I've just noticed the cage door's open."

All possible rabbit refuges were scoured, from inside the grass stacks, to beneath the concrete tubs in the washhouse. Sophia and Colin were near tears, when James arrived home with the rabbit in his arms.

"I found him in the neighbour's garden," he said, then, "What? Yuck," when Colin kissed him.

On the road again

Kathleen looked at Jack's profile as he drove; a smile playing on his lips. There was a sense of calm about him; like he'd soaked in warm perfumed water. If she told him about Bert's proposition, it could be setting a cat amongst the pigeons.

Kathleen thought back to the previous morning, when she'd snapped at Sophia, for putting on her school clothes, when she knew it was pedal-pushers only on a weekend. "Money doesn't grow on trees," she said, as she'd said too many times to remember and had gone outside to view the previous day's destruction when Bert Taylor rattled up on the footpath.

"Nice haircut," he'd said, indicating the lawn.

"It's punishment for unruly behaviour," she said, and that made him laugh.

The man heaved his weight to one side and dismounted his bike. He wheeled it closer.

"You could save yourself this headache," he said, with a sweeping gesture. "If you are ever thinking of selling the section, let me know. I've been meaning to talk to Jack about it."

"Well, you've talked to me now."

"Will you mention it to Jack?"

"Of course."

*

Jack was nursing his own dilemma, about how, and when to deliver Sylvia's invitation. But for now, he had fishing on his mind, and the grouse meal they'd be eating for dinner.

"Tommy says there's fish aplenty out in the bay."

"So, you're heading out further?"

"Of course."

"Decent of him to lend you tackle."

"Well, he knows how we're situated."

Doesn't everybody, she thought, and pondered further on

Bert's proposition. No more forest of weeds. No more of Colin's damn holes in the back section. Money could go on the mortgage, leave them with extra for the week: for the boys' bikes, which they'd been begging for, for ages. Maybe the girls could start dancing, and Colin have music lessons …

The children leapt from the truck when the doors opened and headed up the sand dunes like sniffer dogs.

Jack carried the hamper, shooing his wife on ahead. There was a surprise waiting at the boat shed, which, knowing Kathleen, would either be accepted with grace, or not.

"Morning, all," Tommy called, a smile on his face and the dinghy already on the ramp. There was movement behind him in the shed. "Moira," Kathleen said. "Seems I'm the last one to know anything around here." Red-haired Moira, clasped a freckled hand on Kathleen's arm.

"It was a last-minute thing. Mavis and George said they'd mind the children, so I came."

"You're lucky to have family close by," she said.

Jack observed his wife. Kathleen still suffered from her solitary upbringing; her lack of siblings and friends. It was good to see her with Moira and smiling.

Fish and friendship

Moira and Kathleen kept the dinghy steady while the men arranged themselves inside. Tommy took the oars and Jack their fishing gear. James helped push the boat out. Colin, seated, decked in a lifejacket, waved with his arm kept close to his body, having found, and read *Boating Etiquette* during the week. He was certainly dining out on his 'little genius' status.

"They'll be fine," Moira said.

"Who said I was worried?"

"Mum."

"Sophia."

"I want to go swimming."

"Good idea," Moira said. "Let's get changed."

Kathleen had brought along her Box Brownie; and once the children were in their togs, she posed them in a cluster against the dressing sheds.

"You jump in there with them," said Moira. "I can take your picture."

Kathleen buttoned the shirt dress over her togs and stood with her children. She'd loved having her photo taken as a younger woman, when her waist was described as 'tiny'. But the extra pounds since childbirth added to her girth and an increasing dislike of it.

It was good to be in the sea, however, buoyed by the salty water. Floating on her back, James ahead, and Sophia behind, trying out backstroke. Moira was in the shallows, keeping an eye on Bev.

When Jack stepped from the dinghy, he had to rub his eyes. Kathleen was some yards up the shoreline, on her knees beside Moira, scooping sand into a yellow bucket. The children were busy applying shells to a rather large castle. He put two fingers to his lips and whistled. Heads turned. The children came running. Kathleen and Moira stayed put.

A little faith might be nice, he thought. "Colin," he said, "help us out with the fish."

Tommy had one bucket out on the sand. "Here," Jack said, reaching in to take the weight off Colin's load. "Thanks, son."

"Think we were lucky to stay upright, Jack," said Tommy. "Great catch alright."

Kathleen at Oriental Bay

Bev had her fingers in a bucket, giggling when a fish squirmed. "Yuck," said James. Sophia wouldn't look at the fish at all.

It was the women who filleted the fish, once the men had gutted it, although Moira whispered to Kathleen 'she'd have done a better job'.

Tommy and Jack cleaned out the boat, letting the boys help with the hose. When Colin squirted James it was over, to a chorus of 'it's not fair'.

They fried up kahawai and tarakihi as the sky deepened. "The sun's changed colour," Sophia yelled, and the family oohed and aahed as it hovered beyond the horizon – a gorgeous red-orange globe. Tommy hung up two Tilly lamps and lit the wicks, sputtering light on the family's excited faces. Each held an enamel plate with tomato slices, waiting for a fillet to be flipped their way.

*

Jack was the only one awake on the way home, the truck lights picking out the curves of the road; highlighting the odd cow or sheep still grazing. He'd suggested Kathleen climb in the back with the children and had flicked a couple of rugs over the lot of them. They were asleep within minutes. A light snoring, the odd settling of limbs, were music to his ears as he turned towards Hayward's Hill.

Cat among the pigeons

He drove home from the book-stall the following day, finding it hard to concentrate after his distracting morning. The railway line had recently been electrified and extended, and old Jackie boy had just been asked if he'd like to run the new station's bookstall. 'We should be up and running in two years,' Mr Patterson, the NZR official had said. The cogs were turning, slotting into place; if he was a gambling man he'd have stopped at the TAB and placed a hefty bet.

Bert was pushing his bike along Gard Street; lengths of wood strung from seat to handles.

"Can I lighten your load?" Jack called, pulling into the shoulder.

"I'll leave that one to God. But thanks for asking."

"You should get yourself a truck, Bert; do yourself a favour."

"That reminds me. What did you think about the section proposal?"

Jack scratched under his hat. "Must've missed something."

"Kathleen not tell you?"

He shook his head.

"Time for a cuppa?"

"Yep. Why not?"

"Head on in," he said, "I'll catch you up."

Gene Kelly and white lies

Kathleen wasn't yet home, which left Jack able to scrounge around for the phone book. The Atkins's number was there, as he'd hoped. Okay, Jack, get this over with. He dialled the four numbers and waited. And waited. Bugger. He only had five days to sort this. "Oh. Hullo."

"Hullo. To whom am I speaking?" He liked a well-spoken woman.

"It's Jack McPhee."

"Is everything all right, Jack?"

"Well yes, and no. I completely forgot I was taking Kathleen to her sister's Sunday."

"And so... you can't come around?"

"I'm sorry, Sylvia."

"Things are complicated sometimes – I understand."

He would have liked to ask her what she meant by 'things' and what had happened to her husband, but that would be too brazen. And, for all that he was in a betting mood, he wasn't about to ruin his run of luck. It was time to account for more than his actions.

Bert's suggestion of selling off the section was not as daffy as the man. Jack sat at the kitchen bench, with his Ready Reckoner and a notebook, and taking the pencil from behind his ear, began to do some sums. He began, as natural as breathing, to conjure up a new scheme. This was going to be the acme of all schemes, he thought, as he put the pencil through its paces. He headed the notebook with a title and year on the top of each page. The section. The bookstall. The shop. The house. He thumped the bench. I think this is it Jack McPhee, you've come up with a winner.

His thoughts ran something like this: Sell section. Use some of that money to secure lease for a shop next to Joe's, then start negotiations with Bert about the alterations. The plan would have him working at the station bookstall and Kathleen at the bookshop. He would join her there late morning. She could head home in time for the kids. With this in place and a small borrowing against the loan, they could afford to do up the house. The truck would have to go. And, if pushed, he'd forgo his share of the boat-shed. But whoa, Jackie boy, no sense in letting the horse loose from the stable – just yet.

There was just one major hurdle that he could see. Mrs Kathleen Mary Eliza McPhee.

*

"Fancy the pictures tonight?" he said.

"Let me get my breath," Kathleen said. "It's hot out."

Didn't he know it, having left the house, driven to Trentham, bought the tickets, and dropped in on the Reagan's to ask a favour.

"I'll put the kettle on," he said. "And a drink of milk, young lady?" he asked Sophia, taking hold of her hand.

"Yes please, Dad."

"I hope there's a gingernut left." Kathleen said, when they appeared with the tea.

"Lots," said Bev, giving her the plate.

"Gene Kelly. What do you reckon?" Jack said.

She dunked her biscuit in the tea and nibbled it. "I'd love to go to the pictures, but ...?"

"All sorted." He held up the tickets.

"And the children?"

"Ditto."

He set out a tray with cups and biscuits, emptied the teapot and filled the kettle. He wrote a short note to the neighbours, laying out the teeth-brushing and bedtime schedule for the children. In the living room he laid books beside the radio. All bases covered. Exception: his wife.

"They'll be fine," he soothed, and hustled Kathleen out to the truck.

"It's not the children I'm worried about, Jack. It's her. I wouldn't be surprised if she went through my drawers."

He let out the longest sigh. "Honestly, Kathleen, get in would you, before I change my mind."

*

"That Don Lockwood reminds me of you, Jack," Kathleen said, coming out from the film.

"Is that a compliment?" He laughed. "Not sure I could dance like that though."

"You used to be good."

"We both were," he said.

"Except for me being too tall for you." He took her hand, walking away from the streetlight across the car park, remembering how they'd spun around the dance floors in those heady days before marrying. And...one, two, three; one, two, three. He lifted Kathleen's arm, and pulled her in, managing to keep up the three-four rhythm.

"Move over Gene Kelly," someone yelled. And Jack couldn't help himself. *"Just singing in the rain, just singing in the rain, what a glorious..."*

*

They lay awake; at first talking about old times, and the film, when Jack moved closer to his wife, and stroked her shoulder, hoping she'd turn towards him and clasp him as she used to. She murmured, as if asleep, and settled against her pillow. Jack didn't push the issue, or the conversation, and moved to the edge of the mattress. It was her fear of unwanted children he told himself, not a rejection of him. He repeated this, many times over, waiting for the drag of sleep.

Revelations

He was up at five, making tea in the kitchen, when Kathleen, robe pulled tight around her middle, was framed in the doorway.

"I dreamed about the film last night," she said, reaching for a stool. "Wouldn't it be great if life was like that?"

"Getting the girl, you mean?" He cracked.

"Making something creative. I can't explain exactly."

"There's no reason we couldn't start a business together."

"Like sewing ties?"

"You know that was a hobby. And it went well, for a while." Like the dances he'd run in the local hall during wartime. You couldn't knock a guy for trying something new. He'd made a few people happy and that had to count for something.

"Look. I'm serious, Kathleen. Why don't you meet me at the bookstall after ten? There's something I'd like you to see."

*

Jack fidgeted all morning, glancing up as each southbound train applied its brakes and eased up to the platform. He half expected his wife wouldn't come and the shop-leasing dream turn to custard. When the moods came over her, there was no saying how she'd act at any given moment. She'd dress to match as well, in a faded blue dress and grey cardigan with holes at the elbows. Punishing him, and the children, he sometimes thought, for daring to display any happiness. But there she was dressed up to the nines. A warmth swamped through him. Love? Yes, indeed, Jack McPhee. You're a sucker for a good-looking lady.

Kathleen stepped across the shingle in her sandals, wondering what Jack had up his sleeve.

Morning tea. Goodness. He sat her down at a round Formica table and went up to the counter and ordered two slices of lemon cake and a pot of tea.

"Buttering me up, are we Jack?"

"Thought we'd talk."

"Sounds serious."

He shrugged. "You know the shop Joe's taking over? Well, there's a lease up on the bookshop next to his."

"And you thought ..."

"I thought, if you'd let me finish, that it could be a good opportunity for us."

She sipped her tea, sat the cup back in its saucer. "And how would we achieve this exactly?"

Jack pulled out his notebook. "I've been doing some calculations since Bert asked to buy our land." He looked up at his wife and waited. "He said he'd mentioned it to you."

She turned her dark brown eyes to his and smiled. "I must have forgotten," she said. "It was around the time of that grass cutting business. Too much on my mind."

You monkey, he thought. "Well, it's lucky he spoke to me then – and it got me thinking." He laid out his thoughts in broad detail, emphasising the need to talk with the bank manager and lawyer; essential facts to mention if he was to bring Kathleen around. She trusted people in positions of power.

"Not commenting further till I've seen the place," she said.

"That's great. Let's go take a gander then."

The shop was still operational, with plenty of stock. A healthy sign. Jack noted the fixed shelves and display units, which probably would remain. It was in pretty good nick; the walls had a recent paint job from the looks of things. Lino floor, easy to clean.

"That your truck?" the shopkeeper said. "Good business?"

"It's been good to me," Jack said, explaining the history of his library and going around the camps.

"It's a nice shop," Kathleen said, placing an English *Woman's Weekly* on the counter.

The door tinged behind them.

"I didn't have this one," she told Jack. "Lots of children's knitting patterns."

Jack showed her the shop Joe Wong was taking over, with paint pots and trestles inside.

"I said I'd help him out tomorrow, if that's all right?"

"Why shouldn't it be?"

"Right then. Home it is." Kathleen was quiet during the drive, though he felt no trouble brewing.

How wrong can a man be?

"So why didn't you tell me about running into Mr Atkins' daughter?" she said, as they approached Silverstream bridge. Jack had no one-liners to fit this bill. He kept driving praying for inspiration.

"I didn't want to have her invitation misconstrued. No. That's not it exactly. You can get pretty jealous ..."

They were alongside the shops, and Jack pulled to the curb. "You know, at the river that day, you seemed awfully put out."

"I talked to her this morning. On my way to the train."

"You did?"

"I was reading an advertisement for piano lessons, pasted on the dairy window, when she came out and started talking to me. One thing led to another and we swapped names. That's when you came into the picture. Sylvia seems to think I have a sister, for some strange reason."

Jack engaged the gears thinking there was always some damned hoop to jump through. Bugger, bugger, and bugger.

Silver linings

He always knew his wife was a tricky piece of business, but the way she got herself off the hook and strung him up to dry, was a stroke of genius, or cunning. She was just too damned smart that one, too damned smart, and then, blow me down, she'd manipulated the meeting with Sylvia into a positive for the lot of them.

She was no sooner home when she was on the phone to Mr Atkins, asking about his piano lesson fees. Jack was readying the truck for his Mangaroa run, when she burst outside, grinning like a mad thing.

"He says he'll teach Colin," she said.

God! They hadn't even agreed to the sale with Bert. Talk about jumping the gun. Why couldn't she have taught him piano herself and keep the money for the bike he'd been wanting?

"Kathleen."

"You can get rid of that face, Jack McPhee. Mr Atkins is taking Colin on at a reduced cost. All thanks to you for saving his grandson."

So now I'm in your good books, he thought, but for how long?

"We'll talk it over when I get back," he said, and waved as he rounded the corner. He pulled in to Bert Taylor's drive. If it's good for the goose, it's good for the gander, he thought, leapt out and thumped on Bert's door.

*

He and Bert nutted out plans of their own, with Jack's notes to guide some of the thinking. It took an hour and a half to come up with a way in which each of them would benefit – simply brilliant it was, simply brilliant.

*

Jack picked up a roll of newsprint from the Leader office on his way back through Upper Hutt; it was up there with sweets on a Sunday as far as the kids were concerned. If he was going to get ahead with his talks with Kathleen, he needed the children to be totally absorbed.

Kathleen had prepared a special treat: braised sausages with silver-beet and mashed potatoes, and a semolina pudding with sliced peaches for after. While the children were busily munching in their room, he opened up the conversation, by agreeing to meet the piano teacher. The extended conversation would wait till after dinner; not that he was expecting Kathleen to shoot down the financial plan in its entirety, but he did expect a peppering of bullets.

He helped with the dishes, bathed the girls, and got them in their pyjamas. The boys then bathed, one after the other, both moaning about the lack of warm water, with the old 'it's not fair' tune riffing in the air.

Jack set about lining up the opened newsprint across the passage and tugging on the paper until it had unravelled a good three yards or so. He placed the new box of crayons on the pulled-out end and left the four children to claim their preferred spot on the paper. "Our room," he said to Kathleen, walking ahead of her and flicking on the living-room switch. The single hanging bulb offered enough light for Jack to select a long-playing record. He placed it on the turntable.

"Not jazz, I hope," Kathleen said. They sat facing each other in dull-red armchairs with a cut pile, which Jack now ran his nails along, waiting for the Mario Lanza song to mellow them. He doubted that this evening would be *the loveliest night of the year* as the singer crooned, but like all dreamers, Jack held hope close to his chest. He ran his nails back and forwards on the arm rests, avoiding Kathleen's gaze.

"Now, about Bert's offer," he started, waving his hand in a downward fashion when she went to interrupt. "Let me finish, please. Bert has suggested that he pay for the section in two ways: cash and the renovation of our house – the split is yet to be decided." He leaned down and scratched his shin. "That means, my darling, *if* we decide to go ahead with the shop idea, we should set the wheels in motion pretty soon. Though, remember, we'll have a year to get ready for the change."

"May I speak now?"

He looked up; took a deep breath. "Fire away."

"So...we would use the income for the land to procure the lease?"

"Some of it. Yes. But as I haven't spoken to the owner – yet – I only have Joe's word on what that sum would be."

Kathleen leaned back in her chair and yawned. "I suggest you find that out. I'll be ready to talk when I've heard the full argument."

"How about I make us a cup of tea, and you change the record?" Jack said, rubbing an imaginary badge with his knuckles.

Industry

Kathleen watched Bert Taylor belting in new boundary pegs, because, of course, Colin had put the old ones to much better use as a frame for Kevin Jackson's trolley. It was a craze she wasn't that keen on, for all that she approved of children being active, and independent. The corner where their house was sited, was the culprit, and the slope from Pempsey into Terminus Street was rather too perfect for the neighbourhood boys and their trolleys. But today, the street was quiet, save Bert's hammering – a sound she needed to become accustomed to.

1954 was shaping up very well since she and Jack were getting on better. Having money in the bank was one reason, and also the vegetable garden – or rather, the grubbed land where it would eventually flourish. She looked down on the soil with some satisfaction. Kathleen had been forced to change her attitude towards Bert since selling him the land, as he was shaping up to be a reliable and generous man. He had brought in a digger to work on the newly acquired plot, but insisted he help prepare their garden first.

"The dug ground has to lie fallow over winter," Jack told her, "then re-dug and fertilised in the spring."

"I guess Sister Ignatius taught you that?" she said, knowing full well that most of Jack's education had come from the nuns. He loved those women. Such a contrast to her ill-feelings against the lot of them. Being a left-hander, hadn't helped, nor the daily whacks with a ruler across her small fingers, and the insistence she use the right one. Jack's telling her she should be thankful for becoming ambidextrous didn't change a thing. He was the lucky one.

Jack had already built a compost bin on their side of the fence, made of rough planks, roughly six feet by three. She had instructed the children, on how all raw food scraps would be collected in the bucket out the back, and everyone, yes, everyone, would take turns to empty the bucket in the wooden bin. She left the more scientific part, of how the scraps produced goodness for the soil, to Colin, who true to form had been reading gardening books borrowed from Jack and was keen to educate them all.

To assist the project, she'd bought packets of seed, planted them in dirt boxes, and left them to germinate beside the window in the washhouse. They weren't likely to sprout for a while, but she checked them daily regardless.

The weather was cooling and trips to the beach almost a memory. It was time to get the needles out and start knitting the children's jerseys.

Bright idea

Kathleen's fingers were sore from the knitting. It was like the war

51

effort all over again, churning out Peggy squares and socks by the bin full; not to mention the children the government urged families to have once the war had ended. But knit she must as the next year would probably see her in the shop when time and money would be at a premium. She should be pleased that the shop deal had been confirmed, but that brought changes she was yet to reconcile. The venture couldn't flourish without her input Jack insisted, and she felt the shackles tighten. Every spare penny headed for the bank, and her return to teaching stymied. It was back to scrimping; a verb she knew too much about. Then a thought grabbed her – Sophia could learn to knit. If it was good enough for her at six, it was good enough for her daughter, but Kathleen could not, would not, be her daughter's teacher. Just thinking of fixing her mother's endless knitting mistakes gave her a migraine. There was however, one woman who just might want to help her out: generous, sweet-natured Moira.

*

The frosts had begun early in the valley, mist hugging the ground, which meant cursing most mornings when Jack couldn't start the engine and he had to get the crank handle out. With freezing fingers, he would swing the handle, and again and again until the engine fired. Then there was ice on the windscreen to deal with, when he sorely needed the extra minutes in bed. Finally, he'd flop into the driver's seat, run a handkerchief across his sweating head and lurch off under skies still pink.

For the kids it was exciting; putting dishes filled with water in the yard at night and eating the ice the following morning before school. Kathleen would let them squeal and carry on until her nerves stung with it all and then yell from the back step, "Get to school, right now, the lot of you. Aunt Daisy's on the radio so that means you, are, late. Late. Late."

"Oooh," Colin said, and James laughed, both running off before their mother could reach their backsides. Sophia scurried behind, jumping over the cracks in the footpath, in case she'd end up marrying a rat.

As long as the rain held out, the playground was where most kids gathered, before school and at every break; the boys out on the fields practising their rugby moves and the girls on the asphalt, bouncing ball, skipping or climbing on the jungle gym. "I'm going to knit a scarf," Sophia said, going from one group to another, all engaged with bouncing balls. Everyone ignored her. At home she'd practised bouncing the ball with one hand ten times, then clapping one hand behind her back when the ball bounced up. She was good at that now, and the one when you threw a leg over the ball. But she didn't feel like playing now. All she wanted to do was knit.

"Julie, Julie," she yelled, spying her friend coming across the fields. "I've got something to tell you."

"Is it a secret?" Julie asked.

"Not really. I am learning to knit."

"Can you teach me?"

Sophia wished she could say yes. "I haven't started yet," she said, 'but when I get good, I'll teach you." Julie had already dashed away and was bouncing her tennis ball furiously.

"Come and play, Sophia," she called. But Sophia was sitting on the long bench underneath her classroom daydreaming. "I know what I want to make," she called out.

"What?" Julie asked, bouncing closer.

"A scarf for Daddy."

"That will take you forever," Julie said. "I don't think I want to knit now." And Sophia just smiled.

The long ropes were brought out and the skipping games began – always their favourite *Teddy bear, teddy bear* first – performing a different action with each small verse; *Teddy bear, teddy bear, turn around, teddy bear, teddy bear touch the ground;* the ropes flicking up melting ice from the puddles as they hit the ground.

Sophia usually liked to skip barefoot and didn't mind Jack Frost nibbling her toes. Her feet were always cosy when she pulled on her socks. Better than any heater. But today she was hot all over, and Mrs Connors sent her to sick bay when she got to class. Nurse took her temperature and pulled up her jumper to look at her tummy. "Doctor for you, my dear," she said. "Immediately."

An apple a day doesn't work for some

It was close to five when Jack turned the truck into Gard Street, streetlights already popping on. A light mist covered the windscreen. He wasn't ready for winter. Then headlights flashed behind him. Jack pulled over to let an ambulance pass, wondering what poor bugger that was headed for.

Kathleen was out on the footpath, hunched in her furred brown coat. What a nice surprise, he thought, until he saw the ambulance reversing to their letterbox. "What's happened?" he yelled, thinking the boys must have done real damage in a fight.

"It's Sophia. She's got scarlet fever. Doctor is sending her to the fever hospital."

"Now?"

"Yes, now, Jack." She stabbed a finger towards the house. "Doctor Thompson's inside."

The ambulance staff tailed him through to the lounge, where Sophia sat cocooned in grey blankets. "I'm infectious, Dad." And boy, did she look it. An angry rash covered the exposed skin. Her eyelids were swollen.

"She'll probably be there for a few weeks," the doctor said. "That's the usual run of this virus."

She was six. Just a wee kid. He felt terror tug his chest. "Get better fast, do you hear? Daddy needs his little helper."

"Best not to kiss her, Mr McPhee."

Jack pulled away. His wife was beside him. She pulled her coat across her chest and gave him a look he'd seen her use on the children. "We will manage," she said. "There is no alternative."

*

Kathleen looked through the bathroom window at Sophia standing naked in a bath, while a nurse washed her hair with steaming water and scrubbed her down like she might a grubby blanket. She waited a few minutes and returned to reception.

"Your daughter will be in the ward shortly," the woman said, "you won't be able to go in, but there is a wide window at the end, so you will be able to see her settled." It was just as well she had said goodbye before handing her to the nurse. And there Sophia was, close to the entrance, already propped against pillows in hospital pyjamas, the nurse tucking the sheets in. She looked so small; one of the youngest children there Kathleen thought, looking at the rest of the children in the ward. Boys and girls, in striped pyjamas all, in various stages of sickness she could see. It was just as well Sophia didn't realise she wasn't planning to visit – and it wasn't because she couldn't drive.

Her reasoning went back more than six years, when she was warned the baby might not survive the operation needed in the third trimester. Kathleen hadn't even brought the baby clothes with her; it was that serious the doctors had warned. But tiny Sophia knew better. She survived the upheaval and arrived a week later, to be rushed to the premature babies' unit in the city. Taking the train and bus to the hospital with breast milk when Jack couldn't drive her. She wasn't up for a repeat. Jack did not understand why she clung to past misfortunes, nor her coldness towards the child. He would visit Sophia; she could rely on that.

*

James was returning from rugby practice when he saw the ambulance round the bend. It drove past him. His mother was in the passenger seat. He waved. She didn't.

"Dad. Dad!" he yelled, heaving through the door. "Who's in the ambulance?"

"Boy, am I pleased to see you," he said, hugging him. "It's Sophia. The doctor came, and now she's gone to hospital."

James perked up immediately. "Can we go and see her?"

Jack gathered the children around him on the settee and only then did he notice how muddy James was. "I'm afraid not. She has scarlet fever, a very contagious bug, and the reason the doctor has sent her to a special hospital is, so we don't get it, my boy."

"Are you crying, Dad?"

"As a matter of fact, I am," he said and snuffled in his hanky. "You kids mean the world to me." He sniffed. Worked up a smile. "How about you help me get some dinner going?"

"Spaghetti and tomato sauce?"

"Tinned, or Dad's special?" They scoffed the pasta down like they'd never seen food in a month. He let the boys listen to *It's in the Bag* quiz show for a bit while he got Bev bathed and into bed.

Jack chain-smoked in the kitchen, and drank copious cups of tea, thinking about Sophia and hoping for luck to keep shining on his family. Feeling nauseated, he threw the empty tobacco tin in the rubbish, and coughed his way to the back yard. Tommy had often suggested that he give up the 'coffin nails' as he called them, but it was easy for him to say, he wasn't addicted to the damned things.

Jack waited up until the taxi pulled in and ran out to pay the driver.

While Kathleen bathed, he rustled up sardines on toast for her supper.

"I've been thinking of when I can visit her," Jack said. "Though that will take a bit of juggling."

"It's probably not worth going," she said. "You'll only be able to look through the ward window." He could wave, make faces. Blow kisses. "I'll write to her," Kathleen said. And he would too, to let her know when to expect him.

Ill winds

Then as luck would have it the other three were knocked down like flies, a week after Sophia's admission. Doctor Thompson looked over his glasses at the red-faced trio and announced,

"No school for you lot." He turned to Kathleen. "I think I'd better check you out too, Mrs McPhee – if that suits you?"

"We'll go to my room, if that suits you?"

He did smile, she gave him that. "I'll write out prescriptions for the children, let me know when you're ready?"

She would never be ready when it came to exposing herself, but the doctor was a professional, just pulling up her slip enough to check the midriff. "No spots on you, Mrs McPhee," he said.

"How perceptive," she said, returning a smile.

Kathleen made Colin sleep in Sophia's bed, so she could keep an eye on the lot of them.

"Her bed's awful," he moaned. "It's like a hammock."

She might have clipped him on the ear if he'd not stated the truth. "You can go back to Grandma's old room, once your sister's home from the hospital," she said. "Now jump in, and I'll go get your things."

Some help it was sending Sophia away, she thought. It was now time to ask Moira that favour.

The return

"There, she's all yours," the nurse exclaimed, and passed the blushed-cheeked patient over to her mother, finally dressed in her own fresh clothes. The clothes she had worn to the hospital were disposed of, along with a few books Kathleen had managed to grab before leaving the house. "Sorry about that," the nurse said, "it's policy for infectious diseases. But lovely to have met you and your lovely daughter."

Sophia sat beside Kathleen in the taxi, clutching the baby doll with the blue knitted dress, bonnet and bootees, that she'd just been handed. "Aunty Moira thought you'd like her," Kathleen said, "And – Aunty Moira told me that she'll teach you how to knit."

"She did?" Sophia squeaked. "I can make the scarf for Daddy now."

"He'll like that," Kathleen said.

*

"You smell like, now let me think…wine gums, that's it," said Jack, holding her close, welcoming her home, before scooping her off the taxi seat and carrying her in.

"I'm going to tell everyone at school," Sophia said, "about hospital, my doll – and knitting lessons." Jack looked across at Kathleen, the question hanging between them. "It'll wait," she said. But she hadn't been prepared for Colin's input.

"No one is allowed back at school until the doctor tells us," he announced.

"Thanks for that Colin," Kathleen snapped, as Sophia ran bawling from the room. She followed her into the into the lounge where Sophia had flung herself on the settee.

"Do you want me to help?" Jack yelled out, feeling a headache pending.

"You could get the kids some barley water." They'd borrowed a syphon, to fizz the drink, as it encouraged them to have more liquids. "Here, put my robe on," Jack said, to Colin, helping it around the boy's shoulders. "Thought you could make the drinks."

"Aren't you mad at me?"

Jack laughed. "I've got bigger things to be worried about," he said, and rubbed Colin's shoulder.

The doctor was emphatic that Sophia stay home until the others were on the mend, but had Kathleen told her yet? Jack wandered up to the lounge door and listened. No sobbing. Good. He nudged open the door. Well, well! Sophia was resting against Kathleen's arm, tracing a finger along the words as her mother read from *Heidi.* They'd just started by the sound of it, Heidi had just met Peter.

Jack eased back into the passage, feeling the envelope in his trouser pocket. He perched at the tiny kitchen table and opened the letter. *Dear Dad,* she had written, and just seeing those words made his heart ache. *I would like to come and see you, because I want you to meet my fiancé Graham.* Jeez! She was only – he counted back the years – oh, heavens. Nineteen. *I am in Christchurch now (see above), staying with Mum for the moment. Please let me know soon, so I can make travel arrangements. Always, your Maxine.* Jack folded his arms and leaned on them. Sat back. Rolled a ciggy. He would write and tell her about sickness in the house and say he'd come down to see them later. He knew it would be fine with Maxine, but Kathleen? She hadn't so much as mentioned her name in months, so how the hell was she going to take this news? Ah, there was a phone number. He'd call his daughter. Explain things. He returned the letter to his pocket and went to see the sickly ones.

Ultimatums

Oh, shit! No trousers on the armchair. No Kathleen in bed. It was too early for the copper – surely.

"That you, Jack?"

"Gotta go to the lav," he said. "Urgent." His trousers were on top of the clothes pile. A quick fumble in the pockets turned up a few crumbs and a sixpence.

He sat hunched on the toilet seat, head in hands. Come on, Jack. This is your daughter we're talking about here. He conceded that since Bev had arrived it had been hard. Hard in every respect. Lack of space, money, you name it, Kathleen played every excuse in the book as to why Maxine shouldn't visit. He flushed the toilet, ran his hands under the tap, wiped them on his robe and entered the kitchen. No wife. He filled the jug and stuck in the plunger, putting tea in the pot while the jug boiled. Kathleen came out of the kid's room. "Was Colin okay about sleeping in Sophia's bed a bit longer?"

"What do you think. He won't shut up about the sagging springs."

Jack sighed. Rubbed his forehead. "Tea's made," he said. "Want some toast?" She nodded and sat, undoing the medicine bottles, pouring equal amounts into three small glasses.

"I'll be back," she said.

They sat side by side, Kathleen's hip nudging Jack's. Jack broke the quiet. "That was a good idea putting Sophia in Colin's room. It made her feel special."

"We'll have to make it up to him sometime," Kathleen said.

"The bike perhaps?"

"We've got bigger fish to fry, haven't we?" Jack was baffled, for a moment. He spooned sugar in his tea and took his time drinking, planning that crucial opening line.

"You have read Maxine's letter, I presume?"

"Well, you weren't about to show me, were you?"

"Give me a bloody break, will you?" Kathleen held a finger to her lips, angling her head towards the kids' bedroom. Jack rolled a cigarette and lit it. He exhaled the smoke towards the ceiling. Kathleen went to stand. "I've more to say," he said.

"Well, she's not coming here with the kids all sick."

"She won't be."

"Oh, so you've talked to her already, have you?"

"Kathleen. I. Have. Not. However, I plan to. That is, if you'll return my letter, thank you." He held out his hand and kept it there.

"You'll have to wait a minute." She came up behind him, her breath soft on his neck, reaching forward with the note. Jack smoothed the crumpled paper. He might have turned on a different occasion and wrapped an arm round her waist.

"I shall be phoning Maxine," he said, "to suggest that I go down to meet her fiancé."

"And just how will you afford that, I ask?"

"I don't bloody know. But be damned if you are going to stop me seeing my eldest daughter." He smashed his fist on the table. Stood. Faced her. "I love her. I love all my kids," he said and pushed past Kathleen and out the back door. His hand shook as he relit the cigarette. Damn you, Kathleen, he thought, then, bugger it, and headed back in. "I was eighteen, for God's sake," he said to her back. "A kid. But you know that already. Don't you?" Kathleen stayed there at the sink, her sleeves rolled up to the elbows. Slowly she turned, first pulling one sleeve down then the other and holding her hands behind her.

"Yes, Jack. And I know how your divorce meant that we couldn't marry in the church."

"You bloody well hated the church. You know that too." He was breathing hard; bile rose in his throat. "None of this is Maxine's fault. She does not deserve this shit. And neither do I," he said. "And do you know what?"

"That you've woken the children with all your shouting." Kathleen said, hands on hips. Jack turned to see Bev, clutching Mr Bear in one hand, rubbing her eyes with the other.

"It's all right Bev, Daddy will look after you," he said, putting an arm around her shoulders. He looked back at his wife.

"And the right answer to my question is – that I'll be sleeping in with the kids."

Small mercies

Jack left early and brooded over the previous night's debacle on the drive to work and again on the drive home. He was so dragged down by it all, he didn't feel like entering the house, not knowing how he would be greeted. But home he must go for the sake of the children, who needed him, that he knew. They enjoyed his company, his jokes, his silly songs. His heart ached for all of them.

He called Maxine from a phone box, who was pretty understanding given the circumstances. "I'll try and get down to see you," he said.

And then she'd had surprised him by saying, "I hope you can make it down for the wedding." Oh.

"I'll be there with bells on," he said.

"I'll send an invite," she said, "further down the line." He cradled the receiver until the pips sounded, wishing he had told her how much she was loved.

"Of course, you must go," Kathleen said, when he finally told her about the phone-call "And how's the team?" he said, realising the topic had ended.

"Ready for someone to read to them," she said and smiled. "Mrs Barton brought around the book I ordered. Sophia's been so good with Bev and James; fetching them things, keeping them occupied, playing games." Kathleen reached into her shopping bag, hanging from the wall, and retrieved rather a large parcel. She pulled back the loose wrapping. "The Golden Book of Bible Stories?" he said. "I thought you'd done with religion."

"Not Sophia. She wants to go to Sunday School."

"And you're okay with that?"

"If it's not Catholicism I am."

Well, be damned. "Do you want me to take in the book?"

"I thought we'd leave it until they're ready for school," she said. "And, I've moved Sophia out of Colin's room. For everyone's sanity."

"You okay, son?" he asked, pushing open the door. Colin was sitting up in bed assembling Meccano.

"I got sick of James talking to himself, Dad," he said, continuing to connect a spoke.

"Really?"

"Yes, Dad. He sees things on the roof."

"What kind of things?"

"Don't know, don't care."

"Did you want to share a story with the others?" he asked.

"No, thank you. I'm busy."

Jack patted Colin on the back, praised the motorbike he was making, picked up an anthology of poetry and entered the other children's bedroom. Sophia was in beside Beverly, reading *Goldilocks* aloud. Jack grinned and looked over at James. He was engrossed in a comic.

"Daddy," the girls said, and he bent over to cuddle them.

"It seems I'm redundant this evening," he said, returning to the kitchen, watching Kathleen for a minute as she finished darning the heel of a sock.

"I'll get the bed ready," he said. "Do you want a hottie?"

"Umm hmm." She said, biting the thread.

He pulled out the settee and was flipping a sheet when he spotted a framed picture on the piano. Well, well, well. It was a photo of Maxine at nine or ten, her hair pulled to one side with a ribbon, which he'd kept in his tallboy for the best part of five years. Only one person knew where to find it.

He filled the hottie and popped it between the sheets and changed into his pyjamas. He was going to clean his teeth and stopped. The children's door was ajar, and Kathleen had her head near the gap. "What on earth are you doing?" he whispered.

"It's James. He's talking in his sleep I think." Jack put his head beside Kathleen's. It was like the soundtrack of a western. Lots of clopping sounds, and 'Take that'.

*

Jack cuddled up to his wife, and the pair of them lay like that, each reflecting on possible reasons why James would start talking in his sleep. "Maybe the fever hit him harder than the others," Jack suggested.

"I'll get to the bottom of it," Kathleen said, and Jack had no doubt that she would. He leaned closer, and said, "Thank you," before dropping soundly to sleep.

Fears allayed and gifts given

Just a couple of days later James bounced out of bed and proclaimed he was not only well but incredibly bored. "I want to draw something," he said. Kathleen raided Jack's 'workshop' and returned with two hardboard offcuts and a box of crayons.

"These are yours. But you can't get up until tomorrow," she said, and smiled as James climbed into bed.

Colin was certainly back to his old self, and Beverly too; she caught them in the hallway biffing balls around. It was definitely time for Doctor Thompson's return.

The following morning Kathleen bathed all the children, or rather, she bathed the girls and left the boys to their usual moaning about the bath being cold, etcetera. That was one thing they'd better have renovated along with the house as she wasn't putting up with one small hot water cylinder above the bath for a family of six any more. The basin had no hot tap, and a jug had to be filled from the cylinder over the bath. And the boys thought they had something to moan about.

The girls loved her blowing bubbles, so she allowed them a couple before getting them out. Kathleen rubbed soap thickly on her wet palms, curled up one hand, and blew gently through the gap of forefinger and thumb. The bubble grew large capturing a spectrum in the light and the girls egged their mother to keep blowing till it burst. There was the usual shouting to get everyone ready in time but she was happy with the result. The boys were dressed in virtual uniforms of grey serge shorts and handmade jumpers; the girls in woollen skirts and cardigans. She had whipped the sheets off the beds and washed them early, just managing to hang them out before the doctor pulled up in his black Austin.

"My, my," he greeted them. "Quite a different picture today, thank goodness." He set about checking each in turn. "I pronounce you all well enough to return to school, on Monday."

"Oh. Can't we go today?"

"It's called, 'playing it safe,' my boy. And how have you been, Sophia?"

"I've been helping Mummy," she said.

"She's been a very good girl," Kathleen said.

"And James and Colin, I hope that you haven't been too bored."

"I've been drawing," said James. "And I've made engines with Meccano," added Colin.

"I'd love to see them." Doctor Thompson looked up at Kathleen for her approval. She nodded to the boys.

"You must be pleased this is all over, Mrs McPhee." She thought about the sewing and knitting still to finish. Not to mention the bundles of washing and the fruit that needed bottling, given by well-intentioned neighbours.

"It'll be good to get back to normal," she said, when all she wanted was to lie in bed with the blankets pulled over her head.

"And I've done drawing too," Bev said, when the boys returned with their treasures.

"Go find it," said Sophia. James held out his drawing. "It's what he sees on the roof," his brother announced. Interesting. It was an army. Full of action: horses, soldiers, quite stunning. It was different from other children's art at eight years old; they sought perfection, wanting their people to look life-like, and the results were often static. James' picture was alive; full of movement. She couldn't wait to tell Jack that their youngest son appeared, not only sane, but accomplished.

Colin stepped forward with his Meccano motorcycle. "I'm going to have one when I'm fifteen," he said. "A real one, of course." Not if I have anything to do with it, Kathleen thought.

"It's everyone in bed sick," Bev said. And the doctor admired the picture. "You have a lovely family, Mrs McPhee. And clever with it."

"Thank you," she said. First it was Colin on the piano and now James with his art. Her children just might make something of themselves.

Saturday continued much as usual, with Jack heading off on the library run once he'd finished at the station. Sophia begged to go with him and he felt bad for turning her down but sometimes, time on his own was exactly what he needed.

Come Sunday, Jack and Kathleen lay in bed, until the children's radio programme was switched on in the children's bedroom. They dressed quickly and headed to the kitchen, grabbed the gifts from the high cupboard and ran back to their room. They were like thieves checking their cache, crouched beside the settee arm, as they wrapped the extra gifts that Jack had bought home, and Sophia's Golden Bible. Jack giggled and Kathleen shushed him when they folded their bed back into a couch. "I'll light the fire," he said. "Make it all nice and cosy."

"And I'll make tea. Try and keep things normal." Laughter rolled out from the bedroom. The kids loved this song. She waited for the last verse of the policeman song, smiling in anticipation. *He never can stop laughing, he says he's never tried, but once he did arrest a man, and laughed until he cried. Oh, ho ho ho ho ho ha ha ha ha ha* and the children joined in getting louder with each repeat. Jack made his entrance with the bags of sweets. Some hope of them not being eaten.

She checked the clock. They finished their tea. Jack had a smoke and they returned to their room, Kathleen carrying a tray of toast-sliced bread, butter and jam. The room was cosy. She set the tray alongside the fire and pronged a slice of bread with the long fire fork. "I wonder how long it will take before they work out what we're doing?" Jack said.

"If Colin has anything to do with it, I'd suggest five minutes."

Jack picked up his banjo mandolin and began plucking. "This'll do it." *Curse ya, curse ya, curse ya, that's the worst cup of coffee in Persia. All I want is a proper cup of coffee, made in a proper copper coffee pot.* He paused, hearing the children. Kathleen tossed more coal on the fire.

"Join in kids," Jack said as they swarmed around him. "You know how it goes," and boy did they let rip. *"All I want is a proper cup of coffee made from a proper copper coffee pot. Tin coffee pots and iron coffee pots they're no use to me – if I can't have a proper cup of coffee in a proper coffee pot – I'll have a cup of tea!"*

The girls looked over at their mother. "We're doing toast, we're doing toast."

"What are you waiting for?" Jack said, "I'm starving."

Music brings respite

When Kathleen suggested Jack phone Mr Atkins and see if he could start Colin's lessons, he was in no position to argue. "It might lift his spirits," she said, "take his mind off his leg."

Just a week back at school and Colin was in Doctor Thompson's office, his right foot cradled in the doctor's hand. "You've been doing what, young man?" Colin pushed out his lower lip and tried moving his ankle as directed. "Ouch."

"He was in his socks," Kathleen continued, paused, breathing deeply, "standing on the cardboard inner of a large newsprint roll, working it along the passage like a circus performer."

"An X-ray, to be on the safe side, but I expect that it's just a sprain."

And it was, thank Whosoever, although the ankle required a good deal of elasticised tape wrapped about it and help getting to and from school until the swelling had eased.

"No. You cannot stay home," Kathleen had said, and asked the neighbours to help with delivery and pickup for a few days.

The ankle seemed fine by the end of the week, but Jack didn't think it was the moment to suggest Colin might be wallowing in his predicament. He gave in to his wife's bidding and phoned the piano teacher. Time arranged, 10.30 a.m. the following Saturday, with Percival Atkins insisting he bring the whole family. Indeed.

*

It was only a ten-minute drive, although it might have been a different country altogether: a place of toadstools and children's dreams; sun slanting through a winding avenue of tall pine trees. Jack pulled in beside the letterbox, the ground layered with needles. He looked up at the staggered steps and groaned. As did Colin. "Don't know why you're moaning," he said, "I'll be doing it harder." It was a job more suited to Clydesdales, he thought, easing Colin up each riser so the boy didn't slip. Jack paused on each step; his breathing had become ragged. Kathleen poked his ribs. "Time for more tennis, Jack?"

"I don't need reminding, thank you."

The other children were waiting on the grass clearing at the top.

"There's a dog," Sophia said, and Jack pictured himself fending off the beast, when he saw the black and white spaniel crouched on the porch, with not a hope in hell of bared teeth, fanged or otherwise.

"You're beautiful," Sophia said, and stroked its ceramic head. The green slat door opened, a bell tinkling, and a slim grey-haired man, in a rumpled striped suit revealed.

"I'm guessing it's the McPhee's," he said. "Now, how about I help you there. Colin, I presume?"

"Yes, I am."

"Mr Atkins," Kathleen prompted.

"Mr Atkins."

"Pleased to see you all," he said. "Do come on in."

It took a few seconds to adjust to the artificial light. Wallpaper from a long-past fashion, splashed floral bouquets across the walls. Rag mats covered the floors. On a round mahogany table, sat cups and glasses, a muslin-covered milk jug, a plate of scones, and two small crystal dishes, holding butter and jam. Water was boiling in the distance.

Jack was rather stunned, when a small grey-haired woman walked through the curtained doorway into the main room. Her hair was pulled back into a tight bun, reminding him of a picture book granny. There were no following footsteps and he was surprised at his disappointment. No sign of the enigmatic Sylvia.

"Jenny, meet the McPhee's."

"I'm Mrs Atkins," the woman said, "Percival sometimes forgets to tell people." She smiled. He patted her shoulder. "Jack is the one who saved our Kevin," he reminded her. She approached Jack with her arms extended, took hold of his hands, lifted them to her lips and kissed them.

He blushed. "You're too kind," he said.

Once the tea things were cleared away, Colin was shown the piano. Mr Atkins pulled back the heavy velvet curtain strung across the rear of the room, to reveal a gleaming, black half-grand. The teacher pulled out the long stool and gestured for the boy to take a seat. Colin put his face close to the piano, "I can see myself," he said, and began to play the music he had memorised.

"Play the Handel," his mother urged.

"Only if Dad can sing," he said, raising pleading eyes to Mr Atkins.

"Be my guest, young man."

Colin arranged himself on the tapestry cushion and lifted his hands above the keys. James giggled. Sophia shushed him and Jack stepped forward. "Just the chorus," he said. "This is Colin's day."

"You have a good ear, Colin," the teacher said, the song over. "No doubt about it. Now, see how you fare with this." With a wriggle Mr Atkins settled his narrow form beside the boy's. He spread his long large-knuckled fingers and moved them up and down the keys in a seamless set of scales. "I'll show you the right hand first," he said. "Try and follow the notes I am playing on the sheet music." He continued, slower this time; up and down; down and up. He sat back. "Your turn," he said.

Colin repeated the scale. Note-for-note perfect.

"Did you look at the music, or copy me?"

"A bit of both," he said, turning around and grinning at his family.

Loose ends

"It was good of Mr Atkins to take Colin on," Jack said, a couple of days later. Kathleen was at the sewing machine, pumping that treadle as if her life was hooked up to it, her head forward, her arms pushing the curtain fabric forward every few seconds, letting it fall to the ground.

"Well, I was too busy. Still am," she said.

"You're a marvel, Kathleen." She stopped pushing. Turned around to face him.

"I've heard sarcasm is the lowest form of wit."

"Jeez, Kathleen. Can't a chap praise his wife now?" He moved to the doors; looked out, fiddled with the pencil behind his ear. "Think I'll head outside. Dig me a bloody big hole."

Colin had something here, he thought, shoving the spade hard with his boot heel. A bit of digging, eh? Who would have thought it? No anger in him now. Not a smidgeon. He nudged a stubborn sod from the spade and paused, removing his cap. Sweat trickled down his neck. Then the image of Kathleen stepping into one of Colin's muddy graves flashed before him. He threw back his head and laughed to the sky, scattering a bunch of starlings. He even laughed about the bed-banishing episode. What a cracker she was. He could only hope that the garden would bring her added bounty.

There would be no more digging holes from Colin it seemed. After months of his son being more mole than boy, Colin's rain experiments ended. Now it was music, music, music. He looked over at his son, dark hair flopping forward over the piano keys, practising the scales Mr Atkins had said he should busy himself with until the next lesson. Stuff learning to read music, Jack thought. Looked like cicadas on telegraph lines to him. But the boy had followed his teacher's orders to the letter and for two weeks he had worried those keys until he was note bloody perfect. He hoped this was a good omen.

Warmer times

Spring couldn't have come fast enough for Kathleen. The silver beet was ready to plant out, although the ground needed lime added and another digging over. If Kathleen was happy so was Jack and he helped her with some of the spade work that first morning when the trays were carried around the front. It was hardly ideal to have a vegetable garden aligned with the street, with no buffer into the bargain, but a garden it would be, and magnificent. He set about with string and wooden pegs to ensure the rows were straight. Even without the vegies, it looked good – professional. They had both talked about the best vegetables to grow and there were now many trays of seeds doing what seeds do best. Beetroot, leek, onions and parsnip – it was exciting indeed.

*

While he and Kathleen worked in the garden, the girls scooted up and down the crazed concrete on their trikes. Colin was in a creative phase and was currently building a new trolley for James and himself. Jack was about to check on how much stuff the boy was raiding from his workshop when James appeared. "You better come, Dad, Colin's had an accident."

"What now?" Kathleen yelled.

"He's not hurt," James said. "It's a different kind of accident."

"Right."

James had a grin fit to beat the Cheshire Cat's when Jack caught sight of his brother. Green paint dripped from the boy's head down his front and off the hem of his shorts. Jack looked above him to the shelf where a paint tin lay on its side, a lid on the ground.

"Jeezus!" Colin looked so miserable he didn't even bother to ask what he was up to.

"Grab any old cloth you can find, James." Jack grabbed the turps, pulled a rag off a hook and held it against the opened neck of the bottle and shook. He kicked the rolled tarpaulin open. "Stand there while I try and work this off," he said, and proceeded to soak the cloths and scoop what paint he could off his son's clothes.

Kathleen soon appeared, brought forth by Colin's screaming. Paint had trickled under his shirt and down into his undies. "I'll get a bucket of warm suds," she said, 'because you're not getting in the bath like that."

Colin did persuade his parents he deserved a bath an hour later, while they, along with James' help scrubbed down the concrete. And to think the day had started off so well, Jack mused as he hauled the tarpaulin out the back and got rid of the boy's green footprints.

*

Across the way, Jack noticed Bert leaning on his sledgehammer, looking bloody glum.

"What's up, mate?" he called and walked through the gap in the fence. Jack pulled off his cap and flattened his hair. Bert dropped the hammer.

"Son-in-law has got himself a fancy city job. Can only help me on weekends."

"That's rough."

"You're telling me. If it wasn't for my daughter, I'd tell him where to get off."

"What'll you do?"

"Go door knocking. It's worked before. Must be someone wanting a bit extra."

*

Bert's news bothered Jack. If the daughter's house was delayed it had repercussions down the line for his plans to renovate. He'd ask around his friends too. Never hurt to help a friend. He entered the house just as Colin exited the bathroom, his face red from the ordeal. James sniggered at the end of the hall. No need to canvas the neighbourhood today he thought and without acknowledging either boy he walked back outside to talk with Bert. He was tired of both sons and their stupid behaviour and had thought of a way to tease them.

*

The boys were set the job of carting off-cuts of 4"x2" from Bert's house to the section and stacking them next to the boundary. In a wheelbarrow, mind. When he felt the punishment had met the crime, he joined them on Bert's section.

"How's it going?"

"You've got good workers here, Jack."

"That so?" He winked at Bert. "I guess you'll be wanting to keep them on then."

Jack wished he'd brought the camera. The look on the boys' faces. Oh, this was too mean.

"Next job is to catch as many white butterflies as they can – for pocket money."

"You mean we don't need to do more heavy work?"

"Just the butterflies. That'll do it."

"You got nets, Bert?"

"Just a couple Jack."

"What do you think, boys?"

"Can we start tomorrow?"

Jack and Bert started laughing. Colin and James frowned at each other and shrugged their shoulders.

"Come pick up the nets any time you want," Bert said, wiping tears from his eyes. "We'll work out the price later."

Further construction and disruption

Jack pulled into the railway yards and found a gaggle of men in city attire armed with notebooks. A smaller group were further along hunched around surveying equipment. He guessed it'd be soon, now the bridges for the Silverstream extension were finished. At last. A new station and all that stinky diesel spewing from the old engines a thing of the past.

"Morning, Jack."

"Mr Patterson."

"Going to be a bit of disruption for you."

"I'm used to that."

Patterson grinned. "Should be done by mid '55," he said. "Great to think the trains will run right through to Upper Hutt."

"Yep, great," he said, though he wondered how that would affect his business.

Jack turned back to his truck, climbed up on the seat and sat there, the sun striking his shoulder through the window. There was too much going on altogether, just too much. He wound the window down a touch and rolled a cigarette. It was only a matter of weeks before Bev started school and before they'd time to turn around they'd find themselves in the shop. He felt a flutter in his chest as he exhaled. He coughed. Chucked the butt through the open window and got out.

*

He drove around to see Joe Wong after he'd closed up the stall – more to have a snoop around the neighbouring shop before the move than anything else. Joe took him out the back, leaving a relative to man the store. Every time he saw Joe, there was another nephew or cousin visiting from Hong Kong, all with three letter names like Lin, Loo or Lon.

"You and I be good neighbours," Joe said. "Help keep yard clean." He nodded towards the stack of boxes by the third shop owner's door. "Him in dairy not so friendly."

"Do you know his name?"

"Very strange one, Jack. Ramsbottom."

"You're kidding me."

"And his very big one."

"You are very funny Joe, anyone told you that?"

"Only you."

A large sycamore tree hung over the neighbouring fence. Jack picked up a seed and threw it in the air watching it spiral to the ground. Like my life he thought, like my life.

"I've been thinking, Joe."

"That is funny."

"I'm serious. I'm going to have to sell the truck."

"Can I buy?"

"Thanks, but I'll try and trade it if you don't mind."

"What you get?"

"A good solid car with no holes in the floor."

Goodbye to old friends

Jack climbed behind the wheel of the truck and pulled out the choke. How many times had he done this he wondered, as he pulled out from the curb and headed towards Trentham. He had written notes by Dylan Thomas for his customers and printed off copies on his Gestetner. Kathleen had approved of that, and the prose. He rolled the words around in his head, smiling, delighting in the Welshman's cleverness. *I could never have dreamt there were such goings-on in the world between the covers of books, such sandstorms and ice blasts of words, such staggering peace, such enormous laughter, such and so many blinding bright lights...*

And Jack could never had dreamed the friends he'd make taking his travelling library around the camps and countryside. He wished he could take his customers with him. He whistled out the window to Dave as he drove past the bowling greens. "Catch you up on the way home," he said. "Trentham pub, quarter to five?" A grin and a wave in return. He wouldn't be seeing him so much either, after the move to the shop. This is ridiculous, he told himself; the move is a forward step, not a negative.

Think of what Sister Ignatius used to say when you doubted yourself – 'If anyone can make something of themselves, it is you, Jack McPhee'.

Jack handed out the envelopes to each of his regulars. "If any of you are down Naenae way, do call in, won't you?" he said, knowing how unlikely that was.

"There's a library going up in Upper Hutt I've heard."

"Is that right, Mrs Morris?"

"Once it's passed the council vote."

"Just think of the books you'll be able to read, once that's up and running."

Mrs Gordon put her arms around him. "It just won't be the same Mr McPhee, without you and your truck."

No, it won't he thought, but it would be alright. He waved out the window and drove back to the turnoff, left to Upper Hutt and on to Trentham. He pulled in at the pub, wheels crunching in the metal, looking forward to catching up with his old mate.

"Old times, and all that Jack," Dave said, charging his glass mug against his friend's.

"Appreciate the shout." Jack said. They had just an hour before closing, but quite enough time to talk cars and women. Mostly, it was bluff. During their army days they'd had a few girlfriends – even dated the same one – Lucy Marshall. "We are such clichés," Jack said, rumbling out a laugh. "Are you still seeing ..."

"Elaine Potter?"

"That's the one."

"Going well. How about you and Kathleen?"

"Jack?"

"She's good Dave."

"Hope she'll like working with you?"

"You did, didn't you?"

"Yeah, but I wasn't married to you."

Jack set down his beer. "Don't suppose you'd like to have a gander at a car I'm thinking of buying? It's down at Sykes garage."

"On the way home – why not?"

Making friends with the new

The car was solid all right. A dark green Ford V8 with a bench seat in leather front and back.

"See, Kathleen, the gears are shifted from the column. It shouldn't take long to get used to it."

"I don't plan to drive it, if that's what you're getting at?"

"Never entered my mind."

Colin jumped into the driver's seat after Kathleen's quick departure and immediately began moving gears. "You don't need to tell me," he said to his father, levering himself forward and pushing in the clutch. "Can I drive it to Mr Atkins later?" he asked.

Jack laughed. "We'll wait till you've got your licence I reckon."

"That's years away."

"Like the piano – it takes practice."

Jack drove along the shaded road, remembering that first visit to Colin's teacher. He might ask if he could stay. Like Sophia, he felt Colin copped the short straw from Kathleen. He knew she was pleased about him learning piano but the boy never received the praise his brother did. Jack dwelt on the reasons at times, coming up with the notion it was because one was sporty, the other not. Already James had been in the papers with his rugby team, and cricket. Kathleen loved that; something to crow about. He slowed down and indicated he was turning onto the pine-needled verge. "Did you enjoy the ride?" he asked Colin.

"It was pretty good."

"Better than the truck?"

"You bet."

Jack placed his hand on the boy's arm. "I'll walk you up if you like."

"I'm fine, thanks."

"Okay. I'll do a few jobs and come back for you." Jack watched him climb the first steps up the slope and was about to start the car when he caught sight of Sylvia in the wing mirror. He waited until she was alongside and wound down the window.

"Jack," she said. "What happened to the library?"

"Do you have a few minutes?" He opened the door and Sylvia climbed in.

"I hoped I'd run into you again."

"Likewise."

"I always felt bad about not explaining myself."

"No need to."

"But I do. You see, it's my husband, Ron. I come and see my parents for a break when his mother and sister stay."

"Tricky in-laws, eh?"

"Not exactly. He was injured overseas. How can I say? He gets depressed; thinks he's a cripple."

"I'm sorry. Really sorry to hear that." She's a brave one, he thought.

And next he found himself talking about Kathleen's father being killed in the Great War and the impact that had on the family. "My apologies," he said, pulling back his shoulders.

"It's not like me to rattle on like this."

"You must have needed to talk to someone," Sylvia said, her voice soft, sympathetic.

"Maybe," he said. Close to tears. Embarrassed.

Sylvia touched his hand. "I can see you put others before yourself." He leaned across to open the door.

"It's been nice to talk, Jack," she said, stepping out.

Too nice he thought and settled back to roll a cigarette. "Oh, shit," he said, suddenly remembering the bundles of pamphlets he meant to deliver to various establishments. He was a key distributor for the local Labour Party branch; a commitment, plus others, made at the last meeting. With the house, shop and everything else on his plate, he'd have to rope in the boys for those extra jobs come elections No time to drop them off now, he thought, and lit the smoke he'd rolled.

"A small task for you," he said, as Colin climbed in. "Delivery boy, my man."

Moving on and moving in

Jack didn't let himself dwell on any sweet fantasies about Sylvia. It was a no-go region and that was that. Then it was head down tail up for weeks on end, as he moved the wares from both libraries into the new shop in Treadwell Street and filled up the shelves. Lucky he still had the truck, though it didn't look like his any longer, with the signage painted out. Cream it was now. Old Sykes had insisted on the facelift – or no trade-in. Let him drive the V8 all the while, so no gripe with that. Maybe give him some beers when the deal was done.

Jack roped in his sons for much of the lighter shifting and Joe and Tommy helped out with the rest. Then it was delivery of the stock he'd ordered. Magazines, new books, toys, stationery; enough to make the shop welcoming. Kathleen had been a great help with choosing the stock; having more idea about knitting patterns and that kind of stuff. Thought a week would see them ripe for the opening.

They were at the fold-down kitchen table, ticking off the list of jobs completed. "I think we should make something of the opening," Jack said.

"Like what?"

"You know, balloons, token gifts. A bit of a party."

"Alright in theory."

"That, my darling, I take to be a yes." He reached for her hand and squeezed it. "It's going to be a success. I just know it."

Kathleen knew nothing of the sort; but if it didn't pan out, she wasn't having Jack renege on the promise of her returning to teaching without one hell of a fight.

Routines established and jobs shared

To say a state of happiness was reached would be a stretch too far, although the first months in the shop were almost pleasant, Kathleen thought. Jack set off early in the car, she saw the kids off at the school gate, with James, funnily enough, taking charge of little Bev, seeing her to the classroom door and helping hang up her schoolbag. Facts that Mrs Miller the Junior Mistress had passed on smartly.

At least they were early for school with her needing to catch the 8.40 train to Naenae. It was a push for her get there by 9am, but Jack said, "Let the punters know we'll open at 9.15, but if I have a slack morning I'll open earlier." That suggestion worked out better than Kathleen imagined. She and Jack took turns at preparing sandwiches at night, so they weren't spending precious pennies on bought lunches. She arrived home soon after the children, always finding the boys scoffing back great chunks of bread, thick with butter. Slathers of honey for James; he loved that stuff. Though he did need something to feed his never-ending batteries. He wasn't silly, that boy; had a cup and saucer waiting for Kathleen's arrival, the jug ready but not boiled – as instructed, giving her a quick, "See you Mum," before nipping out the door for sports' practice.

She sipped at her tea, feet up on the chair rung opposite, half listening to Bev's prattle about the day's new vocabulary. Sophia would either be drawing or knitting in the lounge and Colin at the piano, which gave her a little respite before the meal preparation and Jack's return.

Rewards and requests

The benefits from the new shop were slow to accrue, but accrue they did. Once dinner was finished Jack would perch at the table with the Ready Reckoner and on a spare piece of paper worry the pencil lead down to the nub. Kathleen, who hadn't the need of a Ready Reckoner, which both amazed and annoyed him, would casually lean over, press a finger on a total and suggest it may need adjustment.

"Think we could start the girls at dance class?" she asked a few months on. "Things are shaping up better than I expected."

"I thought it was Sophia who wanted to learn." She'd been drawing pictures of tutu clad dancers for weeks and practising steps and arm movements to match; prancing like a baby elephant up and down the passage.

"It seems sensible that they both go," she said. "They can easily catch the train by themselves if they have to." That was certainly true. A short train trip was nothing really, to either girl, and it was a hop, skip, and a jump to the hall for classes. Kathleen had already been in touch with the teacher; no surprises there. Jack felt caught by the net his wife had thrown; cough up for the ballet lessons, or else. However, he wasn't planning to acquiesce to his lovely Kathleen quite so fast. Got to show some mettle, Jackie boy.

"It's only one class a week you know, nothing to get yourself het up about."

"Let me do the sums, okay? And then we'll make the decision."

*

Kathleen must have known he'd finally trip over the surfeit. So, 'Yes' he'd said, and both the girls started ballet. But bugger me, just a month or two in, and Kathleen's at it again, bugging him about James starting piano.

"Does James want to learn piano?" Jack asked. "He's not shown any ability there, as far as I can make out."

"He might. If he's exposed to it. You've seen how talented he is with art."

"Show him a ditch and would he want to dig it?" he said, climbed out of bed, crossed to the French doors and hooked back a curtain. The vegetables were doing well, especially the Brussel sprouts; never seen plants that fantastic, though they were nearly at the end of their run. Attracting attention from the passers-by – the Reagan's from the corner certainly. He chuckled. "They've got the car out, Kathleen." Every Sunday like clockwork they parked their car in front of the garage and just sat there – for hours some days. Maybe they were as nutty as fruitcakes as she'd made them out.

"So, no lessons for James then, is it?"

"Really? Does he need to?" Jack sat down at the piano, opened the lid and plonked at the notes. Sounded worse than a deaf person's first efforts but he kept it up, enjoying the charade. "James gets his musicality from me," he said, swinging to face Kathleen, grinning.

"Two for the price of one, Mr Atkin's said. And you've always liked a bargain."

Jack grabbed his robe from the sofa arm wrapped it tight around him. "I've always liked a bath too. You'll know where to find me."

Jack lay back in the claw-footed tub, wondering when he'd last allowed himself this luxury. By the time he was out and dressed the kids were bashing on the bathroom door. "Go see your mother," he told them. Stupid having the bath really, as he'd be sweaty as a pig being chased by a dog before the hour was up, and fat chance he had at days' end of claiming a second tub of hot water.

Jack knew that this wile would work, and sure enough, he'd scarcely had time to turn half a dozen sods of soil when Kathleen appeared beside him. And as if the air had never been ruffled between the pair of them, she says, sweet as you please, "Haven't we done well with the garden."

Sophia and Beverly appeared all kitted out for Sunday School in white short-sleeved jerseys and pleated skirts. "You look like pretty chrysanthemums from Mum's garden," Jack said, resting both hands on the spade handle. James joined them, looking pretty smart too, in his grey shirt and shorts. "May you sing His praises loud and clear," he joked, for James was in the church choir. He looked around. "Colin not up?" he asked.

"He's playing silly buggers," James said. Kathleen looked up from her weeding, glared at Jack.

"What have I done?"

"The language. It's yours."

"So, what's he up to?" He asked James.

"Lying on the floor. Made me climb over him."

"Off you go," he said to James, "I'll sort it out."

"If you don't, I certainly will," Kathleen piped up. "He's beyond the pale that boy."

The wind changes

"Kathleen. Kathleeen!" She was on her feet, and into the house. Jack had his hands under Colin's shoulders, urging him to sit up. "What's the matter with you?" she said, giving her son a nudge.

"I don't know," he said, crying now. "My legs went all funny."

"You've probably got cramp," she said, indicating to Jack that they lift him up. Colin crumpled back to the floor, sobbing hysterically.

Kathleen put her mouth to Jack's ear. "Get the doctor," she whispered, "I think this is serious."

The next hour was a blur, with Doctor Thompson arriving, checking Colin out from tip to toe, directing Jack to call for an ambulance, and Kathleen to collect his night clothes and toiletries. Jack tucked a checked blanket around Colin then pulled the doctor away from Colin's hearing. "What do you think it is?" he asked.

"We'll run a few tests; there's a number of things it might be."

Jack knew that polio had hit a few families in the area and could feel the noose of terror pulling tight again. Kathleen came out from their room holding her coat and handbag. "I'll call you, when I can," she said, came closer and kissed him. "Try not to worry."

*

He wandered listlessly around the front yard waiting for Kathleen's phone call and saw Brian Johnson crossing the street with his wife Kay. He hadn't seen them since they bought the flooring business. Drove to the city every day, poor blighters.

"We saw the ambulance earlier, Jack. Is Kathleen alright?"

"She's fine. It's Colin who's not."

"Can we do anything to help?"

"Think I'm alright, thanks. Just waiting for Kathleen to call."

Jack could see the Johnson's two boys leaning over their shut gate. He hoped they didn't get this thing and give their parents the jim-jams. He was near crying for the strain of it all; his hands were shaking.

"Colin fell down, didn't he, Dad?"

"Yes, he did, dear. The game finished, is it?"

"James doesn't want to play anymore, and Beverly's grumpy."

Kay Johnson smiled. "Would you like to help me do some baking, Sophia?"

She looked at her father. "I'd like to, Dad."

"She's a good helper alright," he said, putting an arm round her shoulder. "Thanks, Kay," he said, pleased for his daughter as much as himself. She was like a starving chick around Kathleen, hoping for droppings of maternal love. He would do anything to fix the problem, but when he voiced his worries to his wife, he may as well have been speaking to himself, all the good it had done.

The phone. He ran, catching his foot on the carpet runner. He stumbled, righted himself and grabbed the receiver. "Kathleen?"

"Sounds like you need a doctor."

"Very funny. How's Colin? Have they said what's wrong?"

"I'll tell all soon. Are you able to pick me up from the bus?"

"Give me half an hour and I'll meet you at the hospital."

"As you wish. I'll be in reception."

Jack drove down Hutt Road, finding it almost impossible to concentrate on his driving. Sun flickered through the greening willows, dancing across the car's bonnet. "Bugger off," he said. "I'm in no mood for your frivolity."

*

Kathleen moved towards him as he came through the entry, and wrapped her arms about him. He kissed her hair, and guided them to two vacant chairs, away from the glare of fluorescent tubing. "He's going to be fine, the doctors' said. The problem appears to be localised in his left leg; his thigh muscle. And to quote one of them, 'Time will be the healer.'"

"And, is it polio?" Her grip tightened around his fingers.

"Yes; they're fairly certain."

"How is he? Can I see him?"

"He's sedated. They've just given him a lumbar puncture. But we might be able to take a peek at him, through the observation window."

Jack wondered why they had when he saw his son, eyes shut, as helpless as a new-born. The tears were coming. He tugged out his handkerchief and rubbed at his eyes. "He will be fine, Jack. He will be fine," Kathleen said. "Let's go home now, shall we?"

And after James and the girls were in bed asleep, Kathleen and Jack disassembled the settee, pulled back the blankets and crawled in. Just as Jack was about to lose himself to sleep, Kathleen stretched her arm across the bed and cuddled up close to his back. When he stroked her arm, she gave herself to him.

*

They were thrilled when the specialist told them that Colin should be expected to make a full recovery, apart from possible niggles with the weakened thigh muscle. "He might need the crutches for a week or so," he said, "plus a few exercises to help strengthen the leg." The doctor looked directly at Colin. "You'll need to do these daily to ascertain most benefit," showing him a card of diagrams. Colin slumped in the blue-backed chair.

"I don't enjoy exercise," he said, "except ones for the piano."

"What a thing to say," Kathleen said. "You should be thankful your leg's not worse."

"Kathleen," hissed Jack.

The doctor folded his white-sleeved arms. "I've heard that you're bit of a scientist Colin."

"I am."

"Would you be interested in seeing the machines that we use when patients can't breathe on their own?" Colin nodded furiously.

"Are you sure that that's necessary," Jack said. His guts groaned at the thought. He'd seen the poor blighters who'd been stuck in them.

"It would be educational." Kathleen said.

"No patients involved," the doctor explained.

"If you'll excuse me, I need to see a man about a dog," he said. An intake of breath from Kathleen. Jack stretched out his hand to Dr McPherson. "Thanks for delivering such good news."

"My pleasure."

"I'll be back up in a jiff," he told Kathleen. "To give him a hand with those sticks."

A breath of fresh air for all

Jack was wondering how on earth they'd be able to manage the shop with Colin home from school. "Do you think we could take him down with us?" he asked Kathleen. It was either that, or find someone to mind him, or the shop. The kids would all be on holiday soon, an added complication. Kathleen poured tea into his cup.

"You know I told you I'd been speaking with Nora?"

"From Taranaki?"

"Yes. The same. She suggested he stay with them for the holidays."

"I'll give it to you; you're bloody quick off the mark, Kathleen." She smiled. Like a cat with a bowl of bloody cream. "Being on a farm will be good for him."

Jack had to concede Colin's being away might be good for all. Especially Kathleen. You wouldn't have known she had had a kid laid up in hospital the past week, for the lack of dents this made in her routine.

Clearing the head

Moira said she'd mind the other three so he and Kathleen could have a more relaxed trip to Taranaki. If only. Colin was revelling in the attention. And his condition, thought Jack, thinking him well enough to ditch the crutches. But Colin, being Colin, was adamant he couldn't. "Doctor's orders," he said. "If you remember?" Jack looked at his son in the rear vision mirror, sprawled out on the seat.

"I hadn't forgotten," Jack said, laughing. "Though I'm sure it was an estimate, not a definitive quote he gave you."

They passed sheep-covered pasture at first with cabbage trees dotting the fence-line until the road wound around low undulating hills highlighted by splashes of sun. "How about a tongue-twister?" Jack suggested, rolling down the window. He stuck his face out to catch the cool breeze.

"You and Mum are too good at it."

"How about I Spy?"

"Okay."

"I'll start," Kathleen said.

As the *I spy with my little eye* continued Jack found his mind drifting to Maxine. Maybe he could visit while Colin was on the farm. He could leave after work Friday, find someone to cover him Saturday...

"Jack." Kathleen grabbed the steering wheel. "Are you asleep or something?"

"I thought we were going to crash," Colin said.

"A bit melodramatic, son. Though I could be a tad tired," he said, pulling off the road and stopping under a Frosty Jack sign.

"Ice creams anyone?... right. Didn't think there'd be an argument with that suggestion."

They sat on a bench overlooking the river and licked at their cones, Jack mulling over the last time he'd been up this way. Kathleen was boarding with Nora during her country service, when she and Jack weren't officially a couple – that didn't happen until the decree absolute came through. So bloody easy to climb into a marriage but what a rigmarole to climb out. Seven years it took. Seven long complicated years, with him losing Maxine in the wretched tug-o-war.

He manoeuvred his way down the rutted drive to the farmhouse. "Wouldn't want to do this in winter," he said, stopping just short of the front path. Kathleen approached the house first, Colin a few paces behind her. Jack stood by the car door remembering another trip to the country; leaving Maxine with an aunt on her mother's side. Would he ever overcome the guilt? He could see her now: sturdy legs, page-boy hair, plump hand waving. The sooner he went to Christchurch the better.

*

Kathleen was relatively quiet on the return run. "I do hope Colin behaves himself up there," she offered after a while, "I fail to understand what gets into that boy."

"He'll be fine, Kathleen," he said. "Nora's got his number, I'm certain of that." Jack knew that Colin was likely to wallow in the wounded soldier routine, until boredom set in. "We'll phone. Keep a check on him." It didn't bear thinking of Colin on crutches in a paddock full of cows.

Plain sailing

After making his 'spaghetti special' for dinner, and shooing the kids off to their room, he sat at the kitchen table with Kathleen. "The Italians wind it around a spoon like this," he demonstrated. "Makes it easier to eat, supposedly." He slurped at his meal, laughing at his own ineptitude. They adjourned to the living room with a tray of tea afterwards, and sat back in the red armchairs, Jack having told Kathleen he needed to talk.

"Okay if I soak my feet first?" Jack said. "My dogs are barking." Kathleen shrugged.

"I'll get the bowl," she said. "Music?"

"Thanks," he said, lowering his bare feet in the warm water, the strains of Mendelssohn's *Songs Without Words* washing over him. "Now. The visit to Maxine. I could do it in one weekend. Take the train to Wellington Friday. The ferry overnight. Saturday there. Back Sunday night. I'd be back in time to open Monday."

He turned to look at Kathleen. "How does that sound?"

"Fine."

"And… if I took Sophia with me?"

"Even better."

Jack reached for the towel beside the bowl, and dried one foot at a time.

"I suppose you'd like me to do the bookstall Saturday."

He sat up. "Would you?"

"Why wouldn't I?"

"James. Beverly…"

"It's just one morning Jack. I'll manage."

Jack rolled his trousers back down. Padded over to Kathleen's chair. Kissed her on the forehead. "I'll take the water out," he said, "and see if the kids are in one piece." He couldn't pin the unsettled feeling in his gut, but Kathleen was up to something, of that he had no doubt.

To the mainland

Jack walked up the gangway with only one suitcase. It was silly, he told himself, to be upset at Sophia choosing ballet class over this trip with him. Still, it gave him time to gather his thoughts and plan, if that was possible. In his cabin, he splashed water on his face, straightened his tie, pulled a face in the mirror and lurched down the narrow passageway to the dining room. The tables were fixed to the floor; like-wise the chairs. Better not be rough in The Strait this trip, thank you. Jack consulted the menu. Mm! A pie with gravy; a cup of tea after. Now that's the ticket. He pulled a small plain-paged book from his pocket, lay it in front of him and placed his pencil on top. The desire to draw had never left him. But here? He looked about him. Who would care? he thought. Not them, or him, or her come to that, so why don't you sketch something, Jackie boy? It was just the salt and pepper pot to start, and after the meal, he looked down at people's shoes and drew a few of them too. A pair of posh black leathers, and high heels. Got a bit of ankle in with those. A woman with tight blonde curls to his left craned to see what he was doing, He grinned, raised his hand, closed the book, and returned to his cabin. It was good to feel even slightly creative again. Before turning in he squeezed the lumpy parcel in his suitcase. No sharp edges; the china cups were fine.

*

Jack gazed upon Lyttleton Harbour. It was a dynamic port, small, but heaving with activity. You took your chances there wasn't a strike happening; the place was famous for them – and fights. The sky was a mix of streaked mauve and pink; the sun just nudging above the hills to the east. He breathed in deeply. Smelt the salt. I'll never escape the ties of this place, he thought. *It was the best of times, it was the worst of times…* was that how old Dickens put it? He knew how to string words together that's for sure.

He strode across the shingle to the waiting train; just a matter of minutes to Christchurch Station, and Maxine. She'd be there, she said. Would he even know her? She may have grown taller; got fat, or thin? He flattened his hair, adjusted his hat and stood near the window, looking out.

No need for promises

The "Dad," escaping her lips was enough. Maxine had filled out, but it suited her. She looked bonny in a dress of yellow. They hugged as if neither wished to let the other go. His hat dislodged and he reached to catch it. "This is Graham," Maxine said, "my fiancé."

"Pleased to meet you," Jack said, and pumped the man's hand.

"Maxine's got the day planned," Graham said. "Hope you're up for that?"

Jack put an arm around his daughter. "I sure am," he said, kissing her on the cheek, glancing up at the fair-haired fiancé who was a head taller than either of them. He was smartly dressed, in a pale blue shirt, with the addition of a paisley waistcoat. A man who danced to his own tune – and although he could appreciate that – it was what lay behind the attire Jack was more interested in.

"You must be hungry," Maxine said. "Do you have any objections to the station dining room?" He could almost say he loved the place: the dark varnished wood, the circular tables, the white cloths, plus the silver service – that's what finished it off.

"Isn't this posh?" he said, fiddling with the beads on a lace doily. She smiled. A smile which lit up a room Jack thought. She had velvet brown eyes, quite different from his blue-eyed bunch. "You're more beautiful than I remember," he said.

"Thanks, Dad," she answered, her cheeks flushed.

Jack looked at the two of them, clearly besotted with each other. "You'd better look after her, Graham," he said. Maxine giggled, held out her left hand to show the tiny diamond band. He pulled her hand closer, raised it to his lips. "I hope you'll be very happy together."

"We will, I promise." Her eyes glittered.

"You don't need to promise me anything, Maxine," he said, feeling those dratted tears welling up again, thinking of marriage and what it could do to one. Jeez Jack, stop it, right now. "See, you've made your old dad cry," he said, pulling out a handkerchief.

"I intend to look after your daughter, Mr McPhee."

All dressed up for the Queen's visit.

Jack thought it a little early, and somewhat rude if he interrogated the young man on first meeting. At least he had a job, that much he knew. It was a start.

"Now, you two, do I get to know what else you've got up your sleeves?"

*

After dumping his suitcase in a locker, they walked in the direction of Hagley Park. This was one of Jack's favourite places. The daffodils and plum blossoms were over; now just the towering lime trees locking leaves above the pebbled path and bees drawn to their nectar. He stepped back from the engaged couple and watched them walk, Graham shortening his stride to match Maxine's. Holding hands, turning to smile at each other and swinging around to check on him. They headed for a slatted seat across a square of grass and sat beside a pond, the conversation leisurely, veering from any topics which may have marred the day. Jack rolled up his sleeves and fanned himself with his hat.

"Here," he said, reaching into his jacket pocket. "A photo of the kids. Taken when the Queen was passing through." All four had their chests puffed out – like a group of wee pigeons in their finery. "They've grown a bit since then."

"They're lovely, Dad. All dressed up; they look so happy."

"It was a great day. The kids waving their little Union Jacks."

"The girls are pretty," she said. "Sophia's how old now?"

"Going on eight. And Beverly's eighteen months younger. I'll have to bring them down. Show them off in all their glory."

"For the wedding, perhaps?"

"That's right. The wedding. Now, where's it going to be?"

Maxine laughed, pulled at Graham's arm. "Follow us," she said, "and all will be revealed."

As they wound through the paths Jack was struck again by the awe this park brought: the variety of tree species; the size of the trunks; and the sheer foresight of the people in planting them.

He could hear trumpets. Of course! – the band rotunda. Just a small cluster of bugles and trumpets, and a snare drum. He wasn't such a fan of brass; another thing to blame on the army, but give him an old-fashioned pipe band, and he'd be itching to do the fling. "This is where we'd like our wedding ceremony to be," Maxine announced.

"That's different," he said, as if going against the grain was a novelty to him. "We might have a church service too," Graham added, "but definitely some kind of gathering in the park."

"It is a novel, but perfect idea." Jack said, imagining the huddle of guests in their finery; colourful hats at jaunty angles, smiling at the newly-weds.

They bought sandwiches from a stall quite like his own, hosting magazines and papers on wire racks. But here there were tourist brochures, postcards and calendars too. It was a perfect place for visitors he thought. And fathers. He lifted out a calendar, flicking over each leaf. One image appealed above all others: the Avon river, its banks covered in daffodils, trees behind and two people sitting knees up looking out to the sun-rippled water. "I'll take it," he said, to the sturdy red-faced woman, passing over a shilling.

"A souvenir," he told his daughter, which was somewhat outside the truth, for Jack had hatched an idea, which was as usual particularly inspired.

The day was waning into any equally pleasant evening. They meandered around the river bank and headed into the city centre. Jack had forgotten how prolific bikes were in Christchurch and watched them stream by; two, even three abreast. He remembered his brother in his scarred leather jerkin cycling to the tannery on frigid mornings; his scarf wrapped about his face. "That reminds me, Maxine," he said, as if picking up the thread of a lost conversation. "Would you like to see Uncle Henry sometime?" Maxine shared a look with Graham.

"Not this weekend, if you don't mind," she said.

"I'll be staying with him overnight, that's all." Graham was checking his watch again.

"I'm sorry, but I have to push on. I told my landlady I'd be in for dinner, and she doesn't like to be kept waiting."

How very circumspect, Jack thought. "Will I see you tomorrow, Graham?"

"For lunch I believe. I've got that right haven't I, Maxine?"

She giggled, kissed him quickly. "Yes. That's right."

"Maybe I should get home too," she said.

"How about I walk you to the bus," Jack offered.

Maxine clasped his elbow. He patted her hand, and they continued to walk like that, as natural as you please, and Jack couldn't have been happier. "I was wondering if you were going to keep working once you're married," he asked.

"I will for a little while," she said. "We need the money. Besides, I'd miss the girls in the typing pool."

"I was really pleased to hear you got that job. You've done well, Maxine."

"Thanks, Dad."

"Now, Maxine," he said, "Please don't get me wrong. I need to know that you are absolutely certain that Graham is the right man for you." She released Jack's arm, turned, looked directly into his eyes. "I know he is," she said.

Jack watched her go to the back of the bus and take a seat. He blew a kiss, and waved, wishing he had the courage to see her right to her door. It wasn't her mother Gayle he minded so much; it was seeing her with his old mate, Brent. Ha bloody ha. Some mate he turned out to be. They had a son he knew; named him Garth or Garry, something like that. Wouldn't know what to say to any of them, or what to do, if he was left standing on the front step and not invited in.

But thanks to Maxine's chatter while they walked, he arrived at the station with a little more knowledge of the man she wished to marry. Graham was older (by several years); he was a trained reporter (a job, and prospects), was a dab hand at tailoring, and he liked golf.

*

Jack's brother arrived in a Ford Prefect which had seen better days; blue paint scrubbed off in patches showing an orangey undercoat. "How's it going, Henry?" he asked, throwing his case in the rear seat. "No so bad. Kids. Wife. The usual." He looked at Jack proper; gave his stomach a light jab. "Too much of the good life, eh?"

"Too much work and not enough play – that's me – old dull Jackie boy."

He followed his brother into the house. They had always been short buggers, but he'd forgotten how tiny Henry was. Slight, was a better word.

"One knock would see you kiss the canvas."

"I've still got the nimble feet, Jack, don't you worry." Jack smiled, remembering the scraps they got into at the orphanage.

"You always won, Henry. I wouldn't be stupid enough to start that caper." Henry squeezed Jack's shoulder. "It's good to see you. Been way too long, Jack, way too long."

Henry's wife was out at bingo and the children were at the pictures. If he was a sensitive bloke, he'd have thought they were avoiding him. Still, it was good to spend the evening reminiscing with his brother, aided by a little whiskey to loosen their tongues. By the time the others arrived home, Henry and Jack found it hard to string a decent sentence together. "Worse than a couple of kids," Gloria sniffed, "can't leave you alone for five minutes."

"Well, nice to see you," Jack said. "Hope the bingo worked in your favour."

*

The street sweepers had scarcely finished when he was dropped off in the city. Jack breathed in the earthy smell of the dampened bitumen and watched a handful of sparrows enjoy an unexpected bath in the gutter. Jack found himself a cafeteria, and pushed in with his bag, taking a seat at the window. It was always good to watch people come and go; wonder where they had been, where they were going. He ordered a pot of tea, baked beans, toast, tomato and bacon and settled back for his first smoke of the day; thinking of his brother.

He grabbed a tram after and headed out to Brighton Beach. It was a place he knew well; where he'd landed a job in a fish 'n chip shop, right after leaving school. Fourteen he was – hard to imagine now – and that he was running the place before a year was out. He chuckled. Would the building still be there? He scoured the line of brick buildings as the tram rumbled by, and jeez, the old place had survived – and the sign – sun-faded and salt-eaten. Well, well. He alighted at the terminus and strolled around. It was rather lovely he thought, that not too much had changed. The old jetty; the pavilion. A bit seedy, but nothing wrong with that – gave it character. He sat on a bench and checked his watch, tilted his hat forward, and closed his eyes. He had an hour before the tram ride back.

On the waves again

Jack lay on his bunk reliving the weekend. Funny. He could almost see the scenes in sequence; like a movie, or holiday snaps. Maybe that was what James was on about; the 'riding on the roof' as he named it, minus the Western sound track. Hmm. Must talk to him about that. Was the trip a success? He was certainly pleased to have seen Maxine again on the Sunday, and thrilled that she had liked his present. Boy, was the grub good; lamb chops with mint sauce, peas and Red King spuds a bonus. Conversation went better too. Jack told Graham that he had tried sewing and the two chatted about the ties each had made, but the fiancé was clearly the superior tailor. The double stitching on his waistcoat was top notch – his father had taught him that. Adopted he was; never knew his own kin. Could be the reason that he and Maxine were drawn to each other. Two virtual orphans. Being separated from your parents, whatever the circumstances, was shit. And no, there wasn't a better word for describing it. Even his brother, who was alike in looks and not much else, would have agreed with that particular sentiment.

On dry land

The car was parked beside the bookstall, like he left it. He walked around the V8, checking for signs of entry or damage, although leaving the vehicle in view of others should be a deterrent, he thought, though he'd not encountered the 'louts' Joe Wong had mentioned, who loitered around the shopping centre and the local parks.

He went through the usual jobs and banter associated with the stall, but wished to close early so he could get to the shop.

He wanted everything tickety-boo before Kathleen arrived off the train. A bunch of flowers to brighten the place? Not roses. Look where that had got him last time he tried.

"G'day, mate." He called through Joe's back door. The familiar round face appeared, creased into a grin. "Go okay, Jack?"

"Better than okay. Got some fresh flowers, Joe? Thought I'd surprise Kathleen."

"Plenty, plenty. Markets good today"

Jack popped the deep pink phlox in an Agee jar and set them on the far end of the counter. Nice touch, he thought and opened up. He was arranging a new book display when Kathleen appeared, looking relaxed. They hugged. He kissed her cheek. "Nice dress," he said, plucking at the blue cotton.

"Thanks. Just finished running it up."

"It suits you." She placed her bag behind the counter. Sniffed the phlox.

"They're lovely," she said.

"To thank you for covering Saturday." She filled him in about the children's activities, and Colin's reported good behaviour. Sighs of relief all round there. She then asked about his trip away, though any genuine interest was lacking. It hurt. But didn't surprise him. When he pulled out a photo of Maxine and Graham, it was merely adding salt to the same wound, for Kathleen never bothered to pass a comment.

Fortunately, there was a steady stream of custom which took his mind off things. He liked the work and Kathleen did too, he thought. Each had their areas of interest; Jack with the books and comics and Kathleen with the toys, magazines and cards. She was a dab hand at choosing those, plus students' exercise books. He was pleased he got to choose the art supplies, which had helped re-ignite his interest.

After Kathleen left for home, he pulled the calendar from his bag. He matched the colours from the watercolour brochure and wrote the names on the order form. After that, he ordered sable brushes. Winsor and Newton were the best he'd heard, and if he was to achieve a masterpiece, he may as well have those as any.

While the cat's away

Jack opened the door to the sound of the telephone. Sophia and Beverly rushed up the hall. He dropped his suitcase, and flung his arms around them. "My what lovely marshmallows you are," he said, nuzzling their necks.

"Hullo, Dad," James called from the kitchen, "Mum let me listen to her radio."

"What a treat," he said, walking in, patting his back. He pushed the lounge door open; Kathleen was on the phone. She held her hand over the receiver, "I won't be long." Jack wandered over to turn the light on, and happened to look at the piano. A book was resting on the lid. *Piano for Beginners* was its title. He flipped the cover open. James McPhee, he read. For tonight he'd borrow a leaf from his wife's book and not mention his observations. He couldn't bear a confrontation with his meal.

He sat with the girls, hearing them read from their school books. "Look, John, look ..." said Bev. Jack groaned inwardly, having been through the entire *Janet and John* series with the other three kids.

"That was Mr Atkins," Kathleen said.

"Talking over James' brilliance on the piano no doubt." The look Kathleen gave him was priceless, although he wished he'd kept his big trap shut. She dashed off when the phone rang again.

"It's for you," she shouted, "it's Bert, and he wants to talk business." Jack sauntered passed his wife and said, "We'll talk again, my love."

No turning back

"We can start work on your plans, Jack," Bert said. "I'm stalling my daughter's build. Indefinitely."

"Jeez."

"I'm sick of the two of them, to be honest. Can't bloody agree on anything; from the design to the doorknobs. And the labour shortage isn't solved either."

"Sorry to hear that."

"Well. I suggest you and Kathleen get your thinking caps on. You're a dab hand at the pencil, aren't you?"

"Well, yes."

"Give us some idea of what you're thinking. Some rough sketches would help. Once the plans are drawn up proper, it'll be all go Jack."

"So, how long will that take?"

"Give or take a week or two, once I put my draftsman onto it."

"Draftsman?"

"It's a joke, Jack, of course it's bloody well me."

"Silly bugger."

"Now, go talk to your lovely wife. Call me soon, okay?"

"On to it, Bert." Jack retrieved the sketch pad from his tallboy, tucked a sharpened pencil behind his ear, and walked the three plus strides to the kitchen.

The best laid plans

Jack was so pleased he'd taken over the bookshop, for he was easily able to lay his hands on any kind of book he wanted. Books and magazines about colour, design, gardens, you name it and he'd found it. And ordered. This renovation had to work, and he was going to do his best to make that happen. He scoured through the pages in every idle moment, folding down corners, ripping out the odd page. When the watercolours arrived, he began experimenting with small sketches of bedrooms, with different colours on adjacent walls; for this house was going to look up-to-date. A modern bungalow, he'd heard them described; that's what he was after. No trouble lowering the roof, Bert had said. The only thing which couldn't be changed was the size of the foundation. And figuring out how a two-bedroom home could become three, and fit all six inhabitants, plus have a kitchen and living room posed a quandary – or maybe that was a conundrum. But right from that first night when he had sat with Kathleen with a pad and pencil, some small miracle had occurred. He and his wife were actually working together in harmony. Peace almost.

It took them days however, to come up with some configuration they were equally pleased with. Kathleen was rather good at seeing how shapes fitted within a certain space, whereas Jack added the flair. The bathroom would stay put, saving moving taps, etcetera. He already saw how the claw-footed bath could be modernised, by boxing it all around. "See Kathleen," he said, "it would provide a ledge, give you somewhere to keep soaps and so on." It was when they moved on to discuss the children's bedrooms, both of them sighed. They had no choice but house the girls in one room, and the boys in the other. The girls would be fine; but Colin and James together?

"We've managed thus far, Jack McPhee," Kathleen said. "And, as far as I'm concerned, they can like it or lump it."

It was good to be so occupied with the proposed renovation, but difficult to stay positive for weeks on end, waiting for the finished plans. That was the thing; just because the plans were finished didn't spell the end of things. Bert failed to mention it was just the start. "It's like pass the bloody parcel," Jack complained, when Bert mentioned another point the council had queried. It was either the waste water or road access; what was Jack's and what was public property, for somewhere way back whenever, whoever knocked in the boundary pegs must have used a 12" ruler and worn a blindfold.

"Oh, well," Kathleen stated, "at least by the time Bert gets going we'll have sorted out the important stuff."

"Give us time to save for the fixtures."

"Fixtures?"

"You know, taps, handles and the like. I didn't think you'd want to keep the ones we've got."

Kathleen laughed. "I hope that includes the toilet."

"For you, my darling, I'll find the perfect throne."

A soiree of sorts

Kathleen and Jack talked about celebrating Colin's return. "With music. Definitely music," Kathleen said.

"We haven't had a good old knees-up for ages. Better ask your aunts."

"Well, Agnes is always nagging me to visit."

"And Maud?" Agnes's sister.

"You know she won't." True, she wasn't one for social get-togethers. That damned goitre. "What about Violet?"

"I'll phone them." Jack adored his wife's aunts. Agnes was a teacher; a little forbidding perhaps, and a trifle eccentric, but she could thrash out some wonderful tunes on an upright piano. Maybe he should ask her to bring her slide guitar along. She couldn't sing to save herself, but that made it all the more entertaining. But her cousin Violet was as sweet as her name suggested and adored singing. "They'll be here with bells on," Kathleen said, coming off the phone. Oh yes, this would be fun.

"We'd better get the boy back home then," Jack said. "Can't have a party without the guest of honour." But when Kathleen rang to ask about picking Colin up, Nora had insisted that she and Fred would bring him home the following Sunday. "We were planning to visit Fred's sister anyway."

"And the farm?" Kathleen asked.

"All taken care of."

"We expect you in time for the party," Kathleen said.

"Party?"

"A little singing around the piano – a sort of soirée for Colin."

"Pleased I don't have to make that trip again," Jack said. "I think we owe them a gift, don't you?"

"Yes, I do, but what?"

"A big tin of Griffins mixed biscuits? I can get them at cost."

"As long as they're not 'off the back of a truck', like the last lot you brought home."

"I wouldn't dream of it."

Kathleen arched an eyebrow which Jack chose to ignore and looked around the living room, counting on his fingers. So, that was three for a start, plus the aunts. There'd be Moira and Tommy, plus their five kids. It would be a squeeze but the children could go outside; play on the trolleys, skates or whatever.

Next was the list of food needed for an afternoon soirée, everyone's old favourites: saveloys, club sandwiches, brandy snaps. Cream sponges. And, of course, the 'famous' sausage rolls.

Sophia was keen to help with the sandwiches, Kay said she'd make sponges, Moira said she'd bring the brandy snaps. Kathleen thought she had time to make jellies with tinned peaches, or pineapple, which the kids loved, and she'd buy some of those wafer biscuits as a treat.

While Jack was at the bookstall on Saturday, Kathleen got James and Sophia to help her move the furniture to the perimeter of the room and set up a long trestle (borrowed from Bert) in the cleared space in the middle. She searched through the linen cupboard and found the large damask cloth which had never seen daylight, coddled in its original wrap, smelling of mothballs. She flapped it across the trestle, and wondered if her mother would have been pleased at its use. There were a few marks along the folds, but with the dull light and numerous plates, it was unlikely anyone would notice. But then again, Mrs Reagan was popping in. She raced out the back, filled the tub, poured in a little bleach and immersed the cloth. An hour's soak should do it, and another to dry it on the line. She'd save the ironing for the evening.

Overture

Sunday was a beauty. A pure blue sky without cloud. Just birds, swooping and darting; their trills and chirps setting the tone for the day. If Nora and Fred left at eight, they should reach Silverstream by two at the latest. That gave Jack plenty of time to finish the preparations. He had made a programme of sorts; the songs he loved; the aunts' favourites; and had added a selection for the children. He was looking for one more piece of music and fossicked through the stack of classical 78's. He pulled out the Liszt. *Second Hungarian Rhapsody, Part 1*. A nice piano piece to set the mood he thought, and placed it on the turntable.

Then he got a call from Tommy who was called away to look at a house in Titahi Bay. Just two of his tribe would be coming, reducing the numbers considerably, but that was fine by Jack. "Hope it's perfect, for you all," he told him. Thinking ahead to the trips to the beach, and going out in the dinghy.

Everyone else, including the Reagan's, turned up in dribs and drabs as if time was of no importance. The haphazardness of arrivals made the day more interesting Jack thought, lifting the arm of the record player and settling it on the rest, with each fresh batch of visitors. "Don't forget to start the music when you hear the front door," he called to Kathleen. "I'm off to fetch your aunts."

The kids were all outside by the time he returned and were playing some strange game. James appeared to be the ringleader, lining the children up in pairs and getting them to fast-walk along the footpath. Of course. "It's good to see children in the fresh air," Agnes commented, as they headed inside. "James is crazy about the long-distance walker John Reid since he won at the Melbourne Olympics," Jack told her, then called loudly, "Kathleen, Colin's here."

Kathleen had the children inside and sitting on the floor like new entrants, knees crossed, arms folded, and backs straight, before Jack's shoe touched the doorstep. She was at the piano, holding that regal pose. Down her fingers went on the keys and the opening bars of Beethoven's *Fifth Symphony* welcomed Colin and entourage across the threshold. She went from her chair to her son and hugged him. Then embraced her friend Nora. Fred got a tap on the arm. Jack beckoned them into the room, introducing them all round.

"Welcome home, son," Jack said, and patted his back, as he had already taken pride of place at the piano.

"Can I get up now?" James asked. "I want to finish the game."

"And what do you say to your brother?"

"Glad you're better," and charged outdoors.

Interlude

Colin wasn't having a bar of the sporty stuff, and sat flicking through the sheet music. Jack whispered something to him, and Colin grinned. Hard to tell he'd been so ill.

Kathleen bustled in with a filled tray of tea things. "Mum," Sophia called from the doorway, "Can Beverly and I get changed now?"

"Yes, fine. But wait in your room until I call you."

"What's that about?" Jack asked.

Kathleen sighed, "As soon as you put on the Liszt, Sophia asked if she and Bev could dance for everyone."

"And, of course they needed their ballet tunics on. Good on them."

Agnes was holding forth from an armchair, trapping Nora and Fred with a tale he'd heard many times before. "I was on the tram you know, in rush hour, minding my own business, when something sharp poked my side. I spun around and glared at the businessman behind me. Not a blink from the brute. It happened again. Then the tram slowed, and when he passed me, it happened again. I followed him with my folded umbrella and poked him with it as he alighted. "What the hell are you doing?" he yelled. "His face was quite puce, I tell you."

"The punchline, Agnes," Jack called.

"The man disappeared but the poking sensation didn't. In James Smiths' bathrooms, I removed my hat and discovered my hatpin was missing."

"Oh, no," Nora exclaimed.

"Oh, yes," said Agnes. "It had fallen inside my coat and was caught in the lining." Jack applauded. "Love that story, Agnes. Now, how about we eat some of this delicious food?"

Colin was first at the table, stacking up a plate, but what was he doing? Offering it to Nora and Fred no less. Manners. Mm! Something else to thank them for. When all the children had filled their plates, Jack had them sit back down on the floor.

Kathleen sidled up to him, tugged at his sleeve, nodded towards Nora. "They have to leave after this."

"We'll need to start the singing folks. All okay with that?"

"That's what we came for, Jack."

"Now, this may be a surprise to some, but our Colin is to play the first song, as he has become something of a pianist since we last gathered. What are you waiting for singers? Up to the piano."

That wasn't the start of *Lili Marlene*. Jack groaned. Clever work on his son's part, granted. He stood behind the piano stool, expanded his chest, and breathed deeply, waiting for the opening bars of *Where'er you walk*. He bowed from the hips on conclusion, hoping his performance was worth the applause.

"Thank you, Colin," he said. "To all – a short break while we see Nora and Fred off." Jack ushered his son in front of him, gave him the present for his hosts, found the Pimms, set the tray with glasses and returned to the lounge. "A little something to warm the vocals while you wait," he said. Was that 'goody' someone said?

Finale

Everyone gathered around Kathleen at the piano who rattled through the first verse of *Lili Marlene* and paused, waiting for the voices to join in the song.

"First verse again?" she suggested. '*Underneath the lantern by the barrack gate, Darling I remember the way you used to wait ... My own Lili Marlene*'.

"Mum, Mum!"

Kathleen smothered a laugh with her hand. "Another pause, sorry," she said. "You can come out," she called towards the passage, returned to the music and finished the song, ending with an extra flourish.

Colin took the seat once more and played through a piece he'd been practising. He stood, bowing like a virtuoso. When the clapping quietened Jack put on the Liszt and the girls wafted in and around the guests showing off their newly minted chassé, ronde de jambe and jeté. His heart ached for Sophia, for even at this early stage of ballet study Beverly was clearly showing more dexterity; her knees were well turned out and her leap that much lighter. The applause was hearty and Jack whistled loud and long for added effect. "Bravo, he shouted. "Bravissimo."

Not to be outdone, Agnes had taken over the piano and was belting out Violet's favourite, *Come Josephine in a flying machine*. No more Pimms for you, he thought, as Agnes raised her hands high and crashed them down hard on the keys. An hour or so later Jack helped Agnes up into the train carriage and waited until Violet had settled her in a seat.

"Don't worry, Jack," Violet said, as if reading his thoughts, "Len's meeting the train."

"Thank you for inviting me," Agnes said, "I had a jolly fine time."

"It wouldn't have been the same without you," he said.

Jack cuddled into Kathleen that night and whispered, "Now that was fun."

"It was certainly different – I'll give you that."

The encore

Jack was itching to put a long-held plan into action but it had to wait until the end of the week. He felt a little guilty as he turned the *Open* sign to *Closed* on the shop door, as most businesses stayed open late on a Friday, but this really couldn't wait.

He honked the horn several times as he pulled up beside the house. Colin and James appeared on the top step. "Jump in," he called, "We're going shopping."

"I was in the middle of something," Colin mewed.

"Not me," echoed James. Better not spill the beans, son, he thought, wanting to keep Colin's surprise, just that.

"Your loss, James' gain," he said, turning the ignition. That did it. Both boys flung themselves in the back, with the usual pushing and shoving. He looked back to check the car door was closed, and saw Kathleen in the yard, waving. He lifted his hand. She had played her part well.

"Where are we going, Dad?" Colin asked.

"Somewhere you've wanted to go for *ages*." James chimed in.

"The pictures?"

"Sorry, son, I know that you're keen on the new western."

"Not Colin, Dad. It's me who wanted to see *Shane*."

"Apologies all round then," he said. He drove alongside the railway for a bit then headed across the train lines and onto Main Street, pulling alongside the kerb just south of Upper Hutt. Bikes of all shapes and sizes were in stands outside the shop.

"We're here." Jack announced. "Coming in?" He didn't need to ask twice. "Don't fiddle with those," he said, "there's more inside." They sauntered through the shop, eyeing up the new Raleigh cycles gleaming under bright lights.

"These are very expensive," Colin said, pulling out a tag. He and James began checking all the tags along the row. Jack went to the counter and whispered to the green-coated assistant, who pointed to the back wall.

"Boys," he called, "Come over here." Two black Raleigh bikes leaned against the wall. Not new, but still. Beggars and all that. Colin looked at Jack. His father nodded. "They're for you. A bit of a spit and polish should see them right. What do you reckon?"

"Which one's mine, Dad?"

"You choose Colin, James knows you're to have the pick." The boy might have been a doctor, the way he scrutinised the bikes. He thumped the seat, checked the spokes, mudguards, and turned the pedals of both.

"I would like this one," he said, touching the seat. Interesting, Jack thought. It needed more of a spruce up than the other.

"Gee thanks, Colin," James said. "My bike's grouse."

"Yeah, well. With all your sports, didn't think you'd have time to fix one up."

James looked to his father; eyes pleading for his acceptance.

"If that truly is Colin's decision...after all, he's the one who's been in hospital." Jack couldn't see himself being so stoic, or James come to that.

But dear funny boy that Colin might be, he tended to that old bike over the weeks, until there was not one screw, or spoke out of place and polished the seat and frame until it looked brand spanking new. Of course, now James wanted the same attention shone on his choice of bike, but that's where his brother's generosity ended.

A change of plan

Jack called the boys aside just before the summer holidays ended. "We're about to start the house renovations," he said, "and I want a guarantee from you both that you'll help me when called on."

"What do you mean?"

"Well…it may mean that you, Colin, might have to help me out at the bookstall on Saturdays. And both to help around the house more, once the building starts. I can't explain more right now, but I will, very soon.'

"Will I be on my own in the bookstall, Dad?"

"A few times maybe. But I can't tell you exactly."

Colin play-punched James.

"As long as I don't miss cricket," James said.

"You won't, promise."

And then Maxine phoned to say that there was not going to be a wedding in the park after all but a more down-sized one at a registry office, for a couple of very sound reasons. Graham had been offered a job in Oamaru, starting January, and they were getting married as soon as possible. "We've already been down to Oamaru, to check out accommodation," she had burbled, talking about renting, and perhaps buying eventually. He was genuinely pleased for her, for them both, but there was no chance of him being in attendance. There was nothing to be done about it. Nothing.

"Like mother like daughter, wouldn't you say?" Kathleen said, when Jack relayed the phone conversation.

Already crestfallen, he didn't bother to answer, and walked out to the lean-to, gathered his watercolours, pencils, pad and palette, and plonked himself on the grassy bank out back. "There's always bloody something," he muttered, having to retrace his steps to grab his straw hat with the wide, and somewhat unravelled brim. Do not let Kathleen rattle you, he told himself, pulling out the calendar scene from inside his art pad, attached it to the top with the aid of a brass pin and started to sketch the outline.

It took some further shuffling back and forth before Jack was actually ready to paint. Two chairs in line, where he could balance the art pad on one, and sit on the other, with the paints and water-jar on the lip of the old fountain. An hour or so in, Jack spotted Bert down on the neighbouring section. He was with a couple of chaps he'd not seen before. They were pacing out the boundary pegs and scribbling on note pads as they walked around. The scrappy apple tree screened him somewhat as he watched the group wondering what Bert was up to.

And more

"I always knew Bert was not to be trusted," Kathleen said, when Jack had closed the door on his neighbour. "Leading us up the garden path – literally – another six months, and then what?"

"Look on the bright side, love; gives us time to save, maybe we'll be able to get a wringer washing machine. How about that?"

"I doubt it'll bring me considerable joy."

"Lucky you're not Mrs Murphy."

Kathleen laughed. It was good to hear it. And blow me down, she started singing.

"Who threw the overalls in Mrs Murphy's chowder? Nobody knows, but she shouted all the louder. It's an Irish trick that's true and I'll lick the Mick that threw, the overalls in Mrs Murphy's chowder."

"That leaves me off the hook then," Jack said and hugged her until she shook him off.

The waiting

It wasn't so much of a waiting game, as just getting on with each day as it arrived; slapping it about the chops if necessary, when Kathleen had a migraine, the car wouldn't start, or one of the kids got into mischief. Speaking of the last matter. Jack wasn't feeling too flash one Sunday afternoon; exhausted, after cleaning out the junk from the lean-to and loading the trailer for another trip to the dump. He nipped into Colin's room, opening the window before lying down and stretched out on top of the bedclothes. He was asleep in seconds, when a ball flew through the open window and cracked him on the side of his head. He screamed and clutched his head feeling a lump brewing.

Running footsteps outside and down the hall. More screaming – from Kathleen this time.

"What the hell have the boys done now?" she said, rather redundantly, as the softball and Jack's head illustrated the sorry story rather well.

"I'm sure they didn't do it on purpose," he said. Kathleen shooed the girls away, ducked into the kitchen and returned with a damp cloth and Dettol.

"Lie on your side and I'll take a look at the damage."

She dabbed the spot and stood back. "That stings," Jack said.

"Doesn't look life threatening, but we could have it checked out."

"I'll be fine." Jack sat up, looked in the wall mirror, poked out his tongue. "Same ugly mug."

"How about a cuppa?"

"Thought you'd never ask."

James walked into his brother's room, with his friend Mike behind him. "What are you doing in here, Dad?" he asked.

"Recovering from a bash on my head."

James picked up the softball from the floor and stared at it.

"Some silly bugger threw a ball in the window when I was taking a nap."

Jack saw his son flick a look at his friend. "We were playing with the softball, then decided to go play cricket at Mike's. And the window was open..."

Jack sat, dangling his legs off the side of the bed. "Just check no-one's having a snooze next time, okay?"

"I'm really sorry, Mr McPhee," Mike said.

"Please, no tears Mike, I'm fine."

"Dad..."

"It's okay son, truly. But you could wipe that smirk off your dial."

"Something to add, Colin?" Jack said, seeing his eldest enter the room.

"It's James. I bet he thought it was me. Didn't you, James?" Colin shoved his brother and James swung his arm, clipping Colin across his back. "I didn't do it on purpose, so there."

"For Christ's sake bugger off the lot of you. And take the bloody ball with you."

*

Jack joined Kathleen in the kitchen, who was slapping pastry around on the bench. He watched her fold it this way and that, roll it out, chop butter in small pieces, drop it on the pastry and repeat the process. "I'm making flaky pastry," she said, anticipating Jack's question. "Thought we'd have meat pie tonight."

"Would you like me to do that for a bit?"

Kathleen lay the rolling pin down, put her hands on her aproned hips and shook her head slowly. "Just put the kettle on, and I'll join you in a moment."

"Boys in the dog box, are they?"

"You should have given them a slap around the legs, Jack."

"Not my style, and you know it."

Kathleen wrapped the pastry in wax paper and sat it on the bench. "That'll need to sit about half an hour."

Jack poured the tea, helped himself to a vanilla wine biscuit.

"Have you considered where we'll all go once the roof's off?" Kathleen said.

"Not yet," Jack said.

"Oh. So, we should borrow a tent. Pitch it out back?"

"You've made your point." He finished his tea and got up. "We'll work something out." Five minutes later Jack headed down Terminus Street and up Bert Taylor's path.

"Time to work out a schedule, don't you reckon?" he said, removing a pencil from behind his ear, a notebook from his pocket and handing them to the builder.

"You'd be right there, Jack. Better step in."

Surprises of a different nature

Bert did get moving, at a snail's pace, but oddly things were going well with family matters. Savings were on track, and that made Jack happy, what with Colin starting high school and the uniform he'd be needing. And to think that James would be there in two more years. Maxine and Graham were well settled in Oamaru. *The cottage we are renting is small, but nice.* She'd written. *There's just one bedroom, but we have a settee which folds down in the lounge, for when you come down. We framed your painting and have hung it in the kitchen. It is beautiful, Dad. We both love it. Thank you so much.* Jack picked up the photo she had sent of their cottage. A worker's cottage most likely. But tidy. And Maxine on the front porch. He re-read the last paragraph.

I want you to know that Graham and I are expecting. Jack counted on his fingers. He would be a grandfather in a matter of months.

He held out a few days before telling Kathleen, remembering her recent snide remarks about the wedding. But blow me down, it was as if those waters had never been ruffled. "I'd better get some new wool and get knitting," she said. "I think I might make a shawl."

Jack pulled a few notes from his wallet. "Here," he said, and kissed her.

Busy fingers, busy minds

Jack was busy with the Ready Reckoner, Kathleen with a crochet hook most evenings. The children trying out ways to impress each other with peculiar tricks. Right now, they were queuing as one of them stood in the doorframe, hands pressed hard to the frame. "Longer," James urged, laughing as each sibling stepped from the doorway, arms lifting in the air.

"Some education," Kathleen said, hooking down, and along the expanding garment.

"That's a lovely pattern," Jack said. The woollen shawl was lacy, the holes like flowers stacked upon each other.

Kathleen held the shawl to the light illustrating the delicacy of the garment.

"That's pretty, Mum," Sophia said. "Who's it for?"

"Dad will explain."

Jack lowered his pencil, walked across to his daughter and pointed to Maxine's photo.

"Remember I told you about Maxine?"

Sophia looked at the girl with her hair pulled to the side with a clip. "I think so."

"Well. Maxine is married now. It's for the baby she's having."

"I like babies."

"So, do I," he said, cuddling his daughter.

"I'm nearly nine, Dad."

"My big baby, then," he said, squeezing her again. "And, I believe, that it's time for a nearly-nine-year-old to get to bed."

"That goes for all of you," Kathleen said, looking over to James who wanted his siblings to hit him in the solar plexus. "James! You may well have the musculature of a professional boxer, but leave off this crazy stunt. Right now!"

"How about he practises next week's piano piece? It's just past eight."

"I hear you, Jack. James, piano."

Kathleen put the crochet down and bustled the girls down to the bathroom. Colin pushed his fingers to his ears and went to his room. As James plonked his way through *The Volga Boatmen,* Jack felt like copying Colin. This boy held bugger all talent for piano as he'd predicted. James' passion lay with sport and art. And singing.

"Okay son, ready for bed. Read if you want for a while." It would no doubt mean a standoff with Kathleen, but it was past time to end this cacophonic charade. Little did Jack realise that evening, that this wasn't the last he'd hear of James piano pieces, but that delight was a year away.

Guys in the making

As it was Colin's last year at primary school, and possibly his last attendance at a school Guy Fawkes celebration, the family decided to go all out in creating a prize-winning guy for the November bonfire. The preparations were done in secret, well as much as the neighbourhood kids would allow; sneaking around to the back of the house, like young Sherlock Holmes'.

Most families would have a pram, or pushchair to house their stuffed effigies, but the McPhee's no longer had either, and were in the thick of inventing a unique device for their guy.

Of course, Colin found ways of keeping the nosy parkers at bay, by setting string traps around the property. James helped Colin erect a canvas cover over the lean-to's opening, and was given the task, along with the girls, of keeping a lookout for broken string or stricken children.

Saturday. "Dad, Dad," James called, yanking on his arm. "We've got to get going."

Like an army uniform inspection, Jack thought, hauling his braces up, following his sons out the back. He cast a look at the still pink sky before ducking his head and entering his own lean-to. "Oh, dearie me," he said. And there in the trolley, sat a very plump 'guy' sporting a pair of ripped pants, old shoes and shirt. The face, hand-painted on a torn pillowcase looked evil. Dark eyebrows glowering. Thick lips sneering. Well done, however. Colin leaned past his father, and placed a battered black hat on the guy's head.

"So, what do you think, Dad?"

"It's looking good. But how about we add some extras?"

"Like?"

"Hair. Teeth?" Colin looked at his brother and nodded.

"Ok. Wool from your mother, James. Colin and I will stick some teeth on."

"Fangs, Dad?"

"Perfect."

Kathleen appeared waving a hank of dark kinked wool. "Any good?"

"Great," said Colin, taking it from her, and gluing it across the crown.

"Don't forget breakfast you lot, will you?"

The boys were itching to get door-knocking around the neighbourhood, hoping for money so they could scoot down to Mrs Barton's to buy fireworks before the bonfire. They just had time to shovel their Weetbix down, when they heard the shouts of "penny for the guy" from the end of the street. "I think it's Mike and Stephen," Colin said.

"Well, I suggest you head over to the Reagan's first, then up to the square," their father said. "Everyone knows you along there too." He waved the boys off, the guy hunched on black cloth, roped to the front of the trolley, a three-pronged cardboard fork attached to one arm.

"Penny for the guy, Dad?"

"Sure, why not," he laughed, dishing some coins from his pocket. "Go on, you better get out there. I've got to get to going." He reached the car door, shouted to his sons. "Don't go getting any double bangers with those pennies now."

The boys' eyes widened. "We won't, Dad." But he saw the sly glances between them.

"A little bird tells me differently."

He climbed in the V8, thinking about old George Brinkley down Gloucester Street, who complained of bangers been thrown at cars. A group of boys, the story goes. Hiding behind a hedge. Jack wondered how many near-heart-attacks his children were responsible for.

Jack had just turned into Gard Street after work when he spotted the line-up of children with their guys. A quick swoop up Gloucester Street and he was home. "Kathleen, you here?" he called from the door, when she appeared with Sophia and Beverly in the rear. "In the car, pronto."

"What's this?" he said, when Kathleen gave him a small parcel.

"A sandwich to keep hunger pangs at bay."

"Aren't I the spoilt one?"

There was food available at the school as it turned out – the grilled sausages wrapped in bread, were a particular hit. And there were cakes and biscuits aplenty. It was busy alright, with fathers piling the bonfire high with wood offcuts, fallen tree branches, old boxes; basically, anything that would burn. They had set up down the end of the playing field, near the incinerator and the infant block, to access water and hoses. A couple of parents were also volunteer firemen, which gave some feeling of safety. "I'm pleased to see them," Kathleen said, imagining scenes of disaster and devastation.

Parents and children wandered from the main school up the field and took up good vantage points behind the rope cordon. Each guy was pushed in front of its family group to await their fiery fate. Kathleen warned Colin about any trouble-making, but he seemed happy enough standing guard. Clapping began, keeping pace with the chanting of "choose ours, choose ours, choose ours..." as the senior teachers strolled up and down, pausing at each, conferring, writing in notebooks.

The sky was now indigo. Yelling was met by loud 'shushing' from the crowd. Tom Thumbs and Squibs popped and sparked all around. Catherine Wheels spun crazily shooting sparks in all directions, children squealed. Screamed. What was Kevin Jackson up to? "Stop that at once," Kathleen yelled, seeing him throw a lit Tom Thumb at a group of boys. Of course. "James. Colin. Here. Now."

"Mum, we were just playing," James said.

"If there's any more of that sort of 'playing', you'll be heading home. Guy competition or not." Then Roman Candles and Vesuvius fireworks were alight, whooshing brilliantly through the sky, their burnt powder residue stinking and exciting. A sky rocket shot through a low ring of cloud emerging at speed to loud cheering. Then BOOM. Kathleen clapped her hands to her ears. Jack appeared beside her with the girls. "I hate those Mighty Cannons," she said.

"The girls didn't appreciate them either," he whispered, "but they should be fine with these." He dipped his hands in his pockets and pulled out packets of sparklers.

"May I have one too?" Kathleen asked. "Nothing's too good for my girls," he said, placing the thin silver stalks in their hands. "Now, hold them away from your clothes. That's right. Perfect." He lit the tips and the tiny sparks fizzed and popped, illuminating their awed faces. "Watch Mummy write in the air with hers. Good girls; lovely."

Jack looked across where the boys were standing, laughing with their friends. Back from the fireworks, out of mischief. Or so it seemed. He checked his watch and walked towards them. The judging was over in seconds.

"Dad. Mum. We tied first equal!" Thank God, Jack sighed, shaking hands with Stephen and Mike Johnson, and hugging his own boys. The children; clearly more interested in the true highlight of the evening started chanting, "Down with the guys, down with the guys. Burn them, burn them, burn them..." And it certainly didn't take long to get that job done. Flames licked at Jack as he heaved the McPhee guy on the bonfire, quickly retiring to relative safety behind the cordon. With every guy thrown in, the flames shot sky high and settled again until the last guy had had its day and the fire doused. The air reeked with damp smouldering wood-smoke. Jack lit a cigarette as if in communion. "Best get us home," he said. "I don't know about you lot, but I'm absolutely knackered."

"I'm knackered too, Dad," said Bev, and everyone burst out laughing.

"Well, I better give you a piggy-back then," he said, and hoisted her onto his shoulders. Sophia hung back with her brothers who were already eating the sweets they'd won. "Mum, they've got toffees," Sophia said. "Aren't they your favourites?"

A year of significant changes

By the time December rolled around the earth had begun to move, literally. Bert was well on the way to finishing his daughter's house, which was a stone's throw from the back of the McPhee's section, and somehow, from somewhere, he had corralled a team of labourers to speed the project on. It wasn't the McPhees place to question the shift in attitude towards his family, as they could see that their crumbling mansion was finally close to having the facelift it so desperately needed.

Kathleen was able to purchase Colin's high school uniform, which she laid from the shoes up on the living room floor. Black shoes, grey socks, grey shorts, grey shirt and a grey jersey. "How boring," Colin said, although he changed his tune slightly when Kathleen lay the smart maroon blazer and maroon cap on top.

The matter of finding a place to park the family while the major building work was done was part-way solved by the Jones family who had moved in next door eighteen months earlier. Kathleen became friends with the wife Carole, which pleased Jack no end, and he got on with Jim, the mechanic husband well enough. And, yes, Colin thought Jim great, as his relentless questioning about motorbikes and cars were answered; furthering his encyclopaedic knowledge. It was Carole who offered their front lounge as a temporary bedroom. They had just the one child, so 'it is no bother, truly', she'd said to Kathleen. Jack mulled over this offer, and although he thought it generous indeed, he wondered about putting his family in there. They couldn't afford to rent a place, that was true, but he also had no idea just how long the camping over might run.

It was also true, that Carole would have the girls over to play, if Kathleen was late back from the shop. She'd even taken them to a

Front before renovation

134

ballet exam when Kathleen was occupied for the same reasons. It was impractical to ask Tommy and Moira; they were too far away. The Johnson's couldn't help out, with only two bedrooms and a lounge even smaller than the McPhee's. And as helpful as the Reagan's were, they wouldn't wish to be lumbered with their bunch in a house no bigger than a garage.

Speaking of Tommy, the summer had swung around once more, and Jack decided a day out at Titahi Bay would be just the tonic to assuage the current dilemma.

*

Jack faced another problem when the family was gathered on the footpath; of how to fit all four children in the green Ford V8. Kathleen solved it as only she knew how.

"Get in. Stay put, and most of all, shut up."

"But, Mum."

"James?"

"Colin's squashing me."

"Have you lost your hearing?"

"What about sitting Bev beside you, Kathleen?" Jack asked. He put his face closer to hers and whispered. "Stick Sophia in between the boys and that should fix their nonsense."

"Sophia, change places with James, and Bev, you sit up front."

There was a very short round of 'that's not fair' and they were heading towards the coast.

*

The changes in Tommy and Moira's children took Jack and Kathleen by surprise and had them re-examine their own brood more closely. Their friends' boys were taller, and skinny. Not one was podgy; not like her Colin. He'd shot both up and out.

"Before we head to the beach, I'm taking a photo of all you children. Yes, and that means you, Colin and James."

Moira's eldest, Bronwyn, who wanted to leave school, stood sulkily next to Gary and Ron, and Colin stood next to them. James, Sophia and Shirley were the middle row, and at the front stood Gail and Bev. Apart from Bronwyn, who was approaching fifteen, the other children were just a few months apart in age.

"Can I go and see the pigeons, Mum, before we go to the beach?" Colin asked. Kathleen waved the children in from both sides.

"Once I've finished," she said, putting an eye to the viewfinder on her box Brownie. "Cheeese," she said, "and once more for good measure."

Moira took hold of Kathleen's sleeve and led her through the back porch into the kitchen. This was the first state house Kathleen had been in, and in its new-ness it appealed.

"It's very nice, Moira," she said, hoping against hope the kitchen she would soon stand in, would have a similar, just-painted smell. She cast a look at the Formica benchtop which would take pastry rolling well, she expected.

And as if Moira could guess Kathleen's thoughts, she stated, "I hope that you get the workspace you deserve."

Sophia and Beverly were in the front room, admiring the beaten brass dogs on the coal scuttles. The boxes had padded lids, which doubled as seats, and of course the girls had to sit on them. "Look, Mum," Bev said pointing at the wall behind her. Kathleen noted the three ceramic duck's wings out in flight swooping up the wallpaper. Moira was welcome to them.

Kathleen was also not keen on the homing pigeons caged in the back yard. She knew the English kept pigeons as a hobby, and raced the things, but the sight of them in her friend's yard was slightly off-putting. Sophia ran inside when one flew towards the netting, and she could have followed suit. The smell of their dried droppings on the cage floor, was a bit much for the nostrils, so like her daughter she headed back inside. Moira had prepared a lunch of corned beef and lettuce sandwiches, gave wrapped-up ones to the family outside, and returned to sit at the red Formica table with her friend. Moira and Kathleen chatted about the changes in their children, and the changes in their circumstances.

"Do you mind if we go take the boat out now?" Tommy called.

"Not at all," Moira said, glancing at Kathleen. "We'll follow you down in a mo."

The boys ploughed ahead of their fathers through the lupins and onto the sand, striped towels flapping. The girls skipped more than ran, gathering dried pods in their fists which they threw to the sky when the sea came into view. Bronwyn hung back dragging her feet, sighing, flicking her head from side to side like a colt, her blonde ponytail swinging.

"Teenagers," Moira said, "are a different species altogether."

"I am really looking forward to the experience, I don't think, Moira. Colin is a handful as it is."

"Not like missy behind me. It's boys, boys, boys with her. At least Colin has useful hobbies, like music and making things."

Kathleen and Moira ambled without speaking for a while. "Look at us," Bev yelled, from the top of a sandhill. Gail and Bev, towels underneath them slid squealing down the slope. The mothers increased their pace, arriving in the nick of time to see both girls land on the beach with a mighty thump.

"I'd better change," Kathleen said, "if I'm to keep a proper eye on my lot." She'd worn the shirtdress over her togs; a perfect cover-up. "Will you join me, Moira?"

Her friend had already spread a towel on the sand, and a wide-brimmed sunhat on her head. She sat, legs tucked to one side, placed a hand on her stomach and looked up at Kathleen.

"You're not?"

"Yes, I am."

"Lucky last?"

Moira looked up from under her hat. "I don't know," she said, and blushed.

Kathleen swam sidestroke, in sight of the girls, who were engaged in building elaborate sandcastles. There were two bright blue buckets to share, and they took turns at filling them with damp sand. It was quite an assembly line, where the two in front patted the mounds into place. They'd pass the empty buckets to the girls behind them, and wait in line for the buckets to be refilled; resembling a schoolyard ball game. Her thoughts strayed to Moira with another child on the way as she dogpaddled for a bit, then rolled to float on her back. It would never be possible to ask her friend this question, but the thought of what she may answer was a good enough reason to refrain. Was it possible, that Moira enjoyed relations with her husband, didn't bother with precautions, and wasn't bothered about how many children they had? And to think she wasn't even Catholic. Kathleen rolled on her side again, looked out to sea, and saw the dinghy cutting through the distant surf, conveying two seated husbands with Colin between them heading into shore.

Colin leaves primary school behind

Colin started high school, and appeared to settle in. True to form, he applied himself to homework as he had to previous schoolwork, doing exactly the amount required and refusing to extend himself further. With tests he was the same; somehow knowing that he needed to answer just so many questions to achieve a 'pass', and would put his pen down, cross his arms and wait until his classmates had finished.

Kathleen and Jack attended the first parent teacher meeting, where Colin's form teacher presented them with these facts. "If you could encourage him with the importance of following through to the end, he could be top of the class."

"Believe me," Kathleen said, looking towards Jack. "We are aware he can be particular; though that doesn't excuse him – nor his exceptionally high IQ."

"Is that so?"

"It is so indeed, Mr Toogood."

"But, we'll talk to him, won't we Kathleen?"

"We can but try."

Colin proved himself over the weeks, not to his teachers sadly, but to his parents; helping out at the bookshop whenever asked, and at home, packing up books into boxes, ready for shifting. James was as busy as ever with cricket and tennis, but also mucked in to help come Sunday.

A dilemma solved

It was early on a Sunday, when Sophia and Beverly were tucked in their beds listening to the radio, that the telephone rang. Jack recognised Maxine's voice immediately.

"Dad?"

"I'm here."

"Graham and I have been talking about your dilemma …"

"Yes?"

"We would like to have the girls stay with us, while you rebuild the house…"

"You what?"

"The girls, they could go to school here – for a term would it be?"

"Oh, Maxine. I don't know what to say."

"Look. I'm home with Pearl. I could easily walk them to school – it would do me good," she chuckled.

Jack could feel the familiar prickling in his throat. He coughed; cleared his throat.

"I'll talk with Kathleen and call you as soon as I can."

"I'd love the chance to know my sisters, Dad."

Jack swallowed and wiped his eyes, "You are a fantastic girl," he said, and hung up the phone.

Conversation and organisation

Before the school holidays came around, Sophia and Beverly were told of the adventure which lay ahead for them in Oamaru.

Sophia looked across the table at her father, her fork raised, stuffed with peas. The peas fell off. One rolled on the floor.

"The South Island?" she asked, thinking of Mount Cook, Tasman, and the lakes her class had been studying in school.

Jack smiled at her, but his lips were in a straight line, not hooked up at the corners like they usually were when he smiled. "Yes, Sophia," he said, "you will be meeting Maxine." Sophia wanted to feel excited, but couldn't. She looked at her dad but he looked sad. Her mum wasn't looking at any of them. She hooked her apron on the cupboard knob and left the room. The wall shook when she slammed the door and the leather strap swung, left, right. Sophia tried very hard to imagine the girl in the photo with a ribbon in her hair being grownup, but couldn't. Her mother was tall with grey wavy hair, and not very thin, perhaps she'd look like that. She hoped Maxine would smile a lot – and have a pet.

Travelling to Oamaru

I had never been on the Inter-Island ship before. Dad had to hold us by the elbows when we went down the passage because the boat moved and made us walk wobbly. 'You slept like logs', Dad told us when we arrived in Lyttleton Harbour next morning and we laughed. He hauled the leather case with Mum's strap tied right round, up the steps of the huge black steam train, dumped it in the doorway and climbed down again, grabbed our hands and pulled us up, making our school bags bounce on our backs.

When Dad settled back in the green leather seat and opened his newspaper, Beverly and I visited the bathroom. The train rocked and it was hard to walk straight.

I played with the shiny taps and grinned at myself in the mirror while Beverly had a wee.

"Who's the lady we're going to see?" she asked.

"She's our sister," Dad said. Not a whole one like you and me, but a half one."

"Half a sister? How can we have half a sister?" Beverly asked.

"Daddy told me he had a little girl before he had us."

"That's silly. Before us there was the boys!"

"*Before* Colin and James. Before he married Mum."

Beverly screwed up her face. I handed her some toilet paper, helped her off the seat and to wash her hands, and opened the door to the Ladies.

Dad looked up from his paper and said, "Good girls," before leaning across to the window and pushing up the top pane. "Tunnel," he said. And then it went dark. Passengers coughed when the conductor came in and smoke blew along the carriage.

I wanted to ask Dad why we had to leave school to come on this funny journey and not visit in the holidays like other people did. I wanted to ask Dad too why Mum hadn't even said goodbye when we left. But he'd already said it was important and something about making our house different.

Beverly asked him if Mum had measles. "If only it was that simple," he sighed.

It was hard climbing down from the train and Dad had to help us again. I listened to our heels tapping on the footpath as we walked along Thames Street, Dad swinging his heavy case from one hand to the other, while I held onto Beverly's freezing fingers. Ice was lying in puddles. "It's cold here, Dad," I said, but he wasn't listening.

"This is it," Dad said. "This is Eden Street." I wondered about Maxine having pets again. We had a tabby cat, but he was Mum's special friend and he got cross if anyone else came near him. Dad stopped walking, put three fingers to the crown of his hat and lifted it off his head. Beverly and I looked to where he was looking. Three people were on the verandah of a small cream house: a skinny man, a plump lady, and a baby. The adults waved; then the baby. It was pink and quite fat.

"Maxine," Dad called, setting the case down, and unlatching the gate. This Maxine had brown hair and hazel eyes, and she was taller than our father. "Dad," she said, walking towards him, baby on hip, and hugged him with her free arm. He kissed her on the cheek, and turned to us, two children turned to statues. Maxine reached a hand out and stroked my hair.

"She's beautiful," Maxine said, and I could see she was nearly crying. "And so are you, darling," she said to Beverly. Only Dad had ever called us darling.

Beverly whispered, "Where is the girl in the photo?" And the adults laughed, including the skinny man whose name was Graham.

"Would you like to hold Pearl?" Maxine asked me, and I held my arms out for the baby. Pearl. The baby's name was Pearl. This was better than any cat or dog I was thinking, looking down on her soft blonde hair.

Later that day Dad informed us that he wasn't staying long, just long enough to see us settled in. I could feel tears coming and had to sniff to keep them down. "I'm going to miss you, Daddy," I said, and he squeezed me terribly hard. Then while Beverly and I changed into our pyjamas, he helped Maxine fold out our bed, which wasn't really a bed, but the couch in the front room that folded out then lay down, like Mum and Dad's did at home.

When Maxine flapped a sheet and threw it across the bed Beverly giggled. "Climb in if you want to girls," she said. And we lay like two pegs on the cold cotton sheet while she flipped another sheet over top of us.

"Aren't you posh having two sheets?" Dad said, as he pulled the top down over the blankets and tucked the sides in. I ran my feet down the smooth cotton; it felt delicious. We only had a bottom sheet at home, and scratchy grey blankets on top of us. Dad lay alongside me, and reached his arm over Beverly too. The fuzz of his cheek rubbed mine as he spoke, and the next thing I knew it was morning.

The roller blinds were up and sun streamed in the windows. "Pearl's in bed with us." I said, and sat up immediately. Beverly and I held the baby's fingers; or rather the baby curled her tiny ones around ours and grinned at us as if we were monkeys.

"Would you like to help bath her?" Maxine called from the door. Beverly and I answered 'yes' at exactly the same time.

Once Pearl was dressed it was our turn to wash, but in the bigger bathtub. I scrubbed Beverly's back then she scrubbed mine, singing *Row, row, row your boat*. I could hear Graham in the kitchen, and Maxine talking to Pearl, but I couldn't hear the sounds of our father anywhere: the pad of his feet going down the hall, his cough, and his calling out "Rise and shine, sleepyheads," as he passed by our door.

Once we were dressed and the bed turned into a couch again, Maxine sat the both of us down, crouched in front of us and held our hands. "I thought we'd visit your new school today. What do you think?" It was better than telling us our father had left, but not much better.

While the girls were gone

Jack roped the boys into more work once the demolition started; whether it was steadying a ladder, locating more nails, or simply putting on the kettle.

It was a painstaking job, but he and Bert were getting there. It had taken so long to get to this stage, he'd do anything to ensure its finish. And he was doing just that; changing into his old pants the minute he got home, a pencil behind his ear, hat on head, tape-measure in his pocket. He'd be turning into Bert's double if he didn't watch it.

They left the roof supported on the corner trusses, and took the height from the boards underneath, leaving the eleven-foot walls back and front as extra support while the roof was lowered down between them. Bit by bit, weatherboard was cut, or reshaped. Like Bert, Jack was keen to re-use as much timber as they could, to remodel the shortened walls, dependent on its condition.

"These boards will see us both out," he reassured Jack, "you won't recognise them once they're sanded and primed."

It was tricky climbing up and down that ladder, ensuring he didn't come to any disaster. But blow me down, when the rafters were exposed, he caught James fossicking around up there.

"What the heck are you doing?" he said, keeping his voice low in case the boy slipped. James was walking sure-footed across a beam, his arms out sideways, like he did at gymnastics. "Get down right now," he said, pointing across to the ladder. Jack held onto the sides, as his son backed down. "There will be no more of that malarkey," he said. "One slip and it could be curtains for you, my boy."

"Your father's dead right," Bert piped up, having appeared from round the back. "We need you in one piece for the next few months, otherwise this job will never get done."

Jack knew only too well what sacrifices they'd already made, and not a day went past when he didn't think of his two young daughters down south in the cold. He wasn't too concerned about Beverly adjusting to her new surroundings, as she had a more outgoing nature than her sister. Maxine had written that both girls had settled in well, which helped him feel better. With so much work remaining on the building, he couldn't afford to think otherwise.

*

Jack was up and down the jolly ladder, so often, his legs throbbed at the day's end. He'd get Kathleen to fill a basin with warm water and plunge his feet in. "Aah," he sighed, leaning back in a chair. "I couldn't manage without you."

They were now set up in the neighbours' lounge; single beds set against two walls, and a borrowed couch and small table in the middle. They had brought their radio over with them, and the boys were glued to it now, hanging off the ends of their beds, laughing at the *Life with Dexter* show.

"I hope that we're back in our place soon," their mother said, "It is odd, don't you think, trying to avoid the others in the evening?"

"It's as odd as we make it, Kathleen. You wanted us to be as independent as possible, and it is working, I think. The boys seem alright with the arrangements."

"We can't leave the girls down south indefinitely, although it's what we do once they're back, I'm really worried about."

Jack laughed, drew his feet out of the water and wiped them, rubbing each one firmly ensuring they were dry. "How about you ask Carole to put the kettle on? I am sure they're more than happy to share a pot of tea."

Bert up ladder.

House mid-renovation.

*

One night, Bert happened to be biking past the half-renovated house and spotted someone lurking around.

"What the hell are you up to?" he screeched, and a figure raced off through the section and down Terminus Street. Bert peddled furiously around the corner to his own house, grabbed a flashlight and returned. There was nothing obvious missing but enough to cause concerns for safety.

Jack's solution

"There's nothing for it but for someone to sleep there, till the bloody place is secure," Jack told Bert after he learned the news.

"Me, do you mean?"

"Don't worry, I'll set up camp in my own place. We'll be done in a few weeks – right?"

Bert fumbled in his pocket, pulled out his notebook, thumbed through the grubby pages, and finally looked up. Jack aimed for a hangdog expression to meet Bert's gaze. The builder pushed his tongue inside his bottom lip. "It's a promise," he said.

"Shake on it?"

"If you insist," he said, and stuck his roughened paw in Jack's.

*

Sophia wrote regularly from Oamaru, and it was hard to remember that she was only nine, as her writing flowed well, was easy to read; as good as her spelling. He could picture her sitting at Maxine's kitchen table, possibly calling on her to check details.

... Oamaru North school is alright. Beverly loves everything. I don't. My class has Mental Arithmetic in the morning, and it is really hard. I told my teacher I can do the sums if I write them down, and he patted my head. The playground is different from Silverstream school. It has a maypole, like at a gala. I'm not good on the gym bar. The other girls can hook a leg over and go around and around but when I try, I fall forwards and just hang down. The best is when Maxine meets us after school and lets me push the pram...

After a week the girls walked home on their own, Maxine informed him, although Beverly insisted the Sophia needn't hold her hand. He bet she got that stubborn look with the turned-down lip, and chuckled. Such different girls they were, and for all Maxine's assurances to the contrary, he hoped they weren't too much trouble.

Fridays, the girls started dropping into the crockery shop near Maxine's and got to know the shopkeeper, Mrs. Talbot, and just about all of her stock. But it was the families of salt and pepper shakers the girls loved at best. One Friday Mrs. Talbot showed them a man and woman made of wood that squeaked when you shook them. They were rounded like Russian dolls, with red outfits and tiny hats, and Sophia knew that they'd be the present to take home for her mother.

Before dropping to sleep that night, Sophia kept thinking about the old house in Silverstream and wondering why she and Beverly were sent to Oamaru to live with Maxine. It was lonely being away from her family. She dreamed that her mother picked up the wooden salt and pepper shakers and shook them, laughing at the squeaky noise. Sophia and her father had made dinner: lamb chops with silver beet, pumpkin and potatoes and an instant vanilla pudding for after and her mother loving being a guest at her own table. Next morning, she told Maxine about her dream, and Maxine, one hand on her hip looked at her and said, "Well, young lady, how would you like to earn some pocket money?"

"Pocket money?"

"You could help me with some jobs."

So, Sophia got to collect the meat from the butcher's, who would greet her with, "Well, if it isn't Maxine's sister," as she walked in. And, "See you later, alligator," as she left. She liked being Maxine's sister. Sometimes both girls got to walk the baby together and talk about buying the present and going home.

"I'm going to call the shakers Bill and Ben," Beverly said.

"But one's a lady."

"Or … Bill, and Penny." Pearl would add her laughter, and sometimes a wail, like the day they let go of the pram handle and the pram crashed into a hedge. They knew it was naughty to laugh at what had happened but they couldn't help it.

Polishing the floors was Sophia's favourite job. Maxine tied socks around her knees, and showed her how to rub polish on a cloth and to kneel and shuffle, moving the cloth like a window wiper in front. Maxine listened to the radio as she fixed a meal, or did the ironing, singing *Que sera sera,* which was about a girl wanting to know her future. "You'll have rainbows when you grow up," Maxine told Sophia, untying the socks round her knees. "Just like the girl in the song."

Then one Saturday morning, instead of playing games in bed as usual, Maxine told the girls to get dressed, as they were all going for a walk. There was only time for a 'lick and a promise' as their father always said, and the treat of a special breakfast wherever it was they were going.

"Are we going to school?" Beverly asked, tugging Maxine's sleeve.

"Not quite," said Maxine. "You'll have to be patient."

"Would you like to push Pearl?" Graham asked Beverly. She nearly tipped the pram over when she grabbed the handle.

They came to a Private Hotel sign and next thing we were walking down the driveway towards a green painted door. Sophia listened to the gravel crunching as she walked, when the door opened and a man stepped out. "Daddeeee!" Beverly yelled and ran helter-skelter into his arms. "Sophia. Darling, Sophia," he said, putting Beverly down and wrapping his arms around her. "There, there, sweetheart, Daddy's here now. I've come to take you home."

It was almost two days travel from Oamaru to Wellington, by steam train, the ordinary train and overnight ferry. Dad told us we could go to school for the afternoon if we wanted as Mum was working late. So, we went to school, and saw our brothers and our friends, but all day I kept thinking of Mum and when she'd get home and getting the present. Mrs. Talbot had wrapped the salt and pepper shakers in blue paper with gold stars. But I only found out after school was that we weren't going home.

"Sorry, girls," Dad said, "the house isn't quite ready to move into. We're staying next door, just a week or two. It'll be fun, you'll see."

"I wanted to make a special meal for Mum and give her a present and everything." Sophia sniffed, fighting back tears.

"Don't worry," Jack said, "we'll save the treat for another day." He put his finger to his lips, "I won't tell – promise. Now how about I show you where you will be sleeping?"

We said hullo to Mrs. Jones, and ignored Darrin, who was a silly boy and followed Dad into the lounge. I recognized our beds, but not the small couch or the round table. "Where are you sleeping, Dad?"

"Just across the hall," he said, and let us poke our noses around the door. We hung our clothes on a rack in the corner of our room, put our cases under our beds and wandered out to the kitchen.

"That smells lovely," Bev said.

"Gingernuts, just for you," Mrs. Jones said, wiping her hands down a red gingham pinny.

"We'll be back," Jack said, "I'll go show them the house while it's still light."

*

Beverly and I ran outside when we heard the taxi and out to the street to greet our mother. But Mum just grabbed her handbag tight and walked right past. "Perhaps she didn't see us," I told Beverly, taking hold of her hand and following Mum inside. "Here's a present for you," I said, picking up the parcel with the shakers inside. Mum still had on her dark brown coat, and stood really tall, her hands shoved in the pockets. "If you can't remember my birthday, I don't want a present months later, thank you very much," and walked into the parents' room. I heard Mum yell, and then Dad's voice. Beverly and I joined our brothers on the couch and sat not speaking, pretending to listen to the radio. Dad came out a bit later, walked over to us, crouched down, and took hold of our hands just like Maxine did in Oamaru.

"How about you get your PJ's on and I'll tuck you up in a while?" Beverly got down from the couch, but I stayed sitting there. Dad sat in Beverly's spot and hugged me. "I'm so sorry my darling, but your mother's not at all well. I'm sure she'll be feeling much better in the morning."

"I want to go back to Maxine's."

"You will, soon, I promise. But for now, it's off to bed," he said and kissed the top of her head. Sophia lay in the strange bedroom thinking of her big sister, wishing she could be her mother and not just her big sister. When I'm bigger she said against the damp pillow, I am going to earn lots of pocket money and travel to the South Island on the ferry and train all by myself.

Time helps to heal, but the pain remains

Jack tried his best to settle the air after Kathleen's dreadful outburst in front of the girls, by ensuring they stayed out of her way. He wasn't lying exactly by saying Kathleen wasn't well; but as time went by, he saw it was more of the mind than the body. She would have these 'bilious attacks,' and protest that it was a result of migraine, or stomach problems, that caused them. Jack noticed that these 'attacks' often fell on weekends, when Kathleen would take herself off to her bedroom, pull the curtains and close the door. Again, it was Sophia who was affected more than the other three, who all were involved with outside school activities. Sophia did have ballet lessons, that was true on a Saturday, but if Kathleen stayed in her room on a Sunday, Sophia made it her mission to try and help her mother in some way. He remembered before the girls went down south when Sophia made her mother tea with toast and took it to her in bed. "I can't possibly eat that," she said, "it's burnt around the edges."

Jack believed Kathleen's 'bilious attacks' were more about her being depressed; cooped up in the shop, wishing she was anywhere but. But why did she have to upset the children, when it was he she was trying to get at most?

So, Jack hatches another plan

Helping Bert rein in some extra help so the house could be made habitable would be the bait he'd use to help the removal of Kathleen's black cloud. The suggestion of her changing her job, he'd leave to later. Only so much a chap could deal with at one time.

Jack got their bedroom fitted out first, by painting the walls, laying a second-hand carpet piece and moving in furniture. A bed. At last. The plumbing was in, the toilet operable. It was really coming together. He moved fast with the kitchen, laying lino, painting cupboards, and re-installing the stove. The kitchen and living space were open-plan, a unique concept Jack had insisted be implemented, with a narrow wall dividing two open doorway spaces. Yes, he thought, a little smugly, it was time Kathleen saw her almost-ready 'new' home.

Jack took her around the outside, entering through the back door to add to the air of expectation. I can manage with this, she thought, picking her way around the odd pot of paint, checking out the bathroom and the hallway. She looked to the ceiling, so much closer than the old high stud. "No more wind gusting through from back to front," Jack pointed out. "We moved the front door a few feet and added a small porch." She had noticed that from the street, and thought it a good idea. "I can get the children's rooms done in a couple of weeks, then we'll almost be finished." Kathleen looked in their rooms. "I'm going to paint the floorboards and finish the wardrobes so the beds can be moved in," Jack added, "in the colours we discussed."

Kathleen pushed open the last door on the right. Her room. Jack's room. Jack had bought a dark-stained oak dressing table with wing mirrors as a surprise, a job lot, along with the bed and a freestanding wardrobe. He held his breath. Does she love it, or loathe it?

"You've done wonders," she said, turned to him and kissed his check. He placed an arm around her, relaxed his breath.

"I can finish off the walls on the weekends," he said, as they entered the lounge.

"And I'll make some curtains," she said. "Starting with the bedrooms."

"Sounds as if a trip to Evans' fabrics is on the cards then?"

"No time like the present; can we go now?"

An unforeseen delay

The curtains were due to be hung, when the Asian flu hit the community. The boys were thankfully spared, and already sleeping in their old beds in their new room, where Jack had tacked up a sheet for privacy until the curtains were done. Sophia picked up the virus first, and was too sick to move. Beverly thankfully was less ill. But sick nevertheless.

"Let's get Dr Thompson to check the boys as well," Kathleen suggested, with Jack agreeing it made sense. He led the doctor through the newly positioned front door, and into the lounge. Jack supressed a laugh, although the doctor didn't, for the boys looked the picture of good health, sitting upright on the couch eyes shining, both grinning. "I pronounce you both well," the doctor said. "How about that?"

'Whew,' Jack thought, imagining weeks with them confined.

"Can we go now?" Colin asked, before punching his brother on the shoulder.

"You like the 'new' house then?" The doctor asked, having heard of the boys' discomfort about sharing a room.

"It could have been a lot worse, I suppose."

"Not much." James said.

*

"Well, there's nothing to be done, but have the girls stay put until this has run its course, I guess," Kathleen said. Once again,

Carole had come to the rescue, taking care of the girls during the day, and Kathleen looking after them at night. The women would take turns with boiling water, cooling it a little and pouring it in a basin, mixing in the Friar's Balsam mixture and taking it into the lounge. One would prop Sophia up against the pillows, settle the bowl across her lap, have her bend forward, cover her head and bowl with a large towel and have her breathe, in and out, in and out, to ease the chest discomfort. Afterwards, Sophia would flop back on her pillows, her face red with exertion and fever. Then a cloth would be rinsed and squeezed through cold water and placed across her head.

"Do you think there's a reason that Sophia is the first to pick up everything that's going around?" Kathleen asked, half-knowing the statistics around crowded housing situations and poor health. "Don't answer that," she countered.

"Carole and Bill are probably crossing themselves that they escaped this bullet," Jack said, dropping in on the invalids and his wife one night. He could see Sophia was past the worst, but gave her the balsam treatment regardless. He rubbed her arm lying loose on the blanket and whispered through the towel. "I'm painting your room primrose yellow. I hope you like it, sweetheart."

"Beverly told me," she said, as Jack removed the towel. "We both love yellow."

The smell of paint lingers

Finally. The McPhee household were once again ensconced in Number Eleven. Even Jack found it hard to believe the changes, although there was still a little to attend to. The front porch, awaited reinforced glass for its window, and the yard it overlooked remained crazed and broken.

"The outside comes later, I promise," Jack said to Kathleen, speaking from one end of the scrubbed wooden table, two children each side, and Kathleen at the opposite end nearest the corner windows.

"I really like the kitchen," she said, and smiled. The cupboard doors were painted a deep red, trimmed with white, the walls a soft dove grey.

"Lucky I know people," he said, knowing how dubious Kathleen has been about some of his 'friends.' Being a shop keeper had brought him into contact with many salespeople, some of whom dealt in wares outside their legitimate ranges. "I've got some carpet coming my way Kathleen, that I know you'll love. Axminster – how about that?"

She let herself dream for a minute of a house with wall-to-wall carpet, except for the bathroom and kitchen, of course. Fitted carpet. Short pile. She knew the terminology.

"What do you think of this sample?" Jack walked over to the lounge, and came back to the table holding up a piece of grey carpet, short-pile, with a leaf pattern outlined in white.

"That's nice, Dad," from James.

"I like the leaves," from Sophia and Bev.

"Good for lying on," from Colin.

"And I like it too," from Kathleen.

"How about that, folks," Jack said, laying on a thick American accent. "I think we have a consensus here."

"What's a consensus?" asked Bev.

James in unfinished porch.

"Something we all agree on." Jack said, rubbing the pile as if it were Aladdin's lamp.

All hands to the plough

Jack had to drop all work on the house in the weeks leading up to the Elections and had no time to focus on the family. He ran around like a headless chicken sorting out posters that needed for printing for the branch, organising people who could provide transport for pickups in the neighbourhood, to name just a few of the jobs he'd made himself responsible for. He ticked the jobs he'd attended to from the list he had complied. Both the Silverstream Hall and School were where the nearest ballots boxes would be placed, and he still hadn't talked to the hall managers. He leaned back, placed his pencil behind his ear and sighed.

"You can ask for help," Kathleen said, looking up from the books she was marking. "I could phone around. Rustle up some of those lazy members."

"I was dreading doing that."

"And our children could easily do a pamphlet drop."

"Thanks," he said, reaching over to tap her hand.

Election day was like preparing for a school gala: bikes were decorated, flags flew and people laughed and shouted. Everyone in the neighbourhood knew where each other's party predilection lay, as blue or red ribbons streamed from car aerials, and lapels sported dinky blue or red bows. Children ran up and down the footpaths beside the decorated cars, maybe hoping for a glimpse of their local candidate, or to be invited for a ride.

Jack couldn't have wished for a better day; clear skies and not a whiff of rain. Only nine a.m. and he was already warm from his exertions; escorting people between election booths and their homes. He drove around the streets checking on his children, whom he'd tasked to door-knock and give out voting reminders to adults. Kathleen had baked scones which he took down to the party rooms and had himself a cup of tea while he was about it. The nail-biting period was hours away, when he seriously hoped there would be a massive party swing in Labour's favour. Dear old Walter Nash, such a stalwart of Labour. It would be great if he won again; he'd been too long in opposition.

Jack was having a cold beer down in the rooms when the results came over the speakers. Cheers, hugs and the partying started. He excused himself early; happy and exhausted, but thankful people had voted in Labour's favour. Walter Nash, fancy that, New Zealand's new Prime Minister. He would phone through his congratulations to Walter in the morning; the man would need his beauty sleep. Kathleen and the boys were huddled around the radio when he arrived home, listening to the speeches which followed the results. Jack put on the kettle, and brought the pot of tea through to the lounge.

"We won, Dad," Colin said. "That we did, son, and maybe we wouldn't, without you two helping." Jack leaned towards James, head drooping, eyes closed. "Bed now, I think. Time to dream of what tomorrow might bring."

James gains fame

Soon all the McPhee males were glued to the radio in the evenings. British comedians calling themselves The Goons had taken over their lives. Spike Milligan, Peter Sellers and Harry Secombe. They sang, made silly noises and the boys loved them. Their favourite was the *Ying Tong* song, which saw Kathleen flee the living room every time it came on the radio.

"Dad," Colin said, after the song had gone through its very many choruses. "You'd be good as Harry Secombe. I could be Spike, and James?"

"Peter Sellers."

Secombe did have a nice tenor voice, Jack thought. Heard he was professionally trained in opera.

"Okay, Dad, 'from the top' as you say."

"I know all the words," said James.

"That goes without saying." Jack cleared his throat. "Ah ha ha ha ha ha ha," he warbled through an octave, then stood as tall as his five foot four-and-a-half-inch frame would allow. "Right," he said and started. *'There's a song that I recall My mother sang to me'*…

'Oooohhh!' Colin sand in a wobbly sorrowful voice. "That's the off-stage voice," he said.

"You'd know." His father said. "Shall I carry on?" Thumbs up from Colin. *'She sang it as she tucked me in, When I was ninety-three'*. Jack paused. Signalled to his sons. They all chime the chorus in high nasal voices … *'Ying tong ying tong, Ying tong ying tong, Ying tong iddle I po, Ying tong ying tong, Ying tong ying tong* (James went slow, imitating 'Bluebottle') *Ying tong iddle I po'*.

Colin: *'Keep lad up. Keep'*.

James*: 'Keep up lad up'*.

Jack: 'LOOK OUT!'

Colin drummed on his thighs making a running sound.

They sang on … *'Ying tong ying tong, Ying tong ying tong, Ying tong iddle I po, Ying tong ying tong, Ying tong ying tong* (James slows again), *Ying tong iddle I po…'*

Jack clapped the boys on their backs. Laughed. "That was great, sons. Great. But now it's time for bed!"

It was Sophia who broke the news to her parents that James had taken his new-found talent a step further than either of them had ever anticipated. Quite a few steps further than their lounge in fact: he and a couple of classmates were now performers of the *Ying Tong* song, going around classes showing off their antics during school hours.

What next?

"I have been thinking, Jack," Kathleen said, several days later, "that we should start the boys at singing classes. What do you think?" Jack took his pencil from behind his ear and chewed the end.

"I think, that one Goons' song does not a singer make, my dear."

"Of course not. But you know James loves singing. And before you say it. Yes, I admit the piano hasn't worked in his favour ..."

"But singing might?"

"More than 'might'. And that goes for Colin too. He has a reasonable voice. Have you noticed?" Yes, he had noticed. He knew that much was true. He also knew why Kathleen was so keen to push the children to learn one thing after another: these were the very things that she might have excelled at, even made a career of, given the opportunity. Kathleen could play the piano, was proficient enough for primary teaching purposes, but singing she had truly loved. To study music and singing; that had been Kathleen's dream.

It transpired that the boys were sent to a Mrs Bennett in Wallaceville for singing tuition, just a block or two from Colin's school. James leapt at the opportunity, even if it meant accompanying his brother, and readily agreed that his piano lessons should end. Jack never suspecting that the music James had struggled over would soon be given a new lease of life.

*

He had observed Sophia looking over her brother's shoulder when Percival Atkins had taken James through his keyboard paces early on in the piece, but he shrugged it off as a natural curiosity on her part. The true nature of her visual memory came to light a mere week after the singing lessons were confirmed. The family had gathered in the lounge after dinner, when the phone rang for Kathleen. She spoke in a louder-than-usual-voice. His ears weren't the only ones to prick up.

"Oh, is that so, Mrs Campbell? It is good to hear that your daughter wants to learn the piano. You're thinking of buying a new one? Right…"

Jack watched Sophia creep quietly from the room and disappear into her bedroom. Mm, he thought. Something's crook in Mussel Brook. He leaned against the wall divider and tried to pick up the thread in Kathleen's conversation but she replaced the receiver in its cradle, turned her head towards the passage and yelled, "Sophia!" And in a more *sotto voce* to Jack, said, "No, you stay here."

Sophia looked on from the hallway.

"Did you know that our Sophia is teaching music these days?" she said, catching her daughter's gaze. "Is that right Sophia?" he asked, wondering how on earth this story would pan out.

She looked directly at her father; tilted her chin. "That is right, Dad". I've been teaching Susan. But Kay wants to learn too."

"Pray tell, just what do you teach Susan?" her mother asked. Sophia folded her arms firmly across her chest.

"I teach her the tunes in the *Piano for Beginners* book."

Jack smiled. "James' book?"

"Yes. When he's at sport, which is every single day. I practise the piano. And when I showed Susan the tunes I could play, she begged me to teach her, so I did. Her mother thinks I'm a very good teacher. She gives me tea and cake when I have finished."

"Well, well, well," her mother said. "This is most ingenious of you Sophia, but it can't continue."

"Kathleen…"

"If you're as good as others think you are, it's about time you played something for your family." With poise Sophia lowered herself on the seat and lifted the lid of the piano.

Changes afoot

Before Kathleen got to enrol Sophia with the boys' new music teacher, she was sent a letter asking if she wished to renew her teaching registration. This was the type of pivotal moment Jack had envisaged, when Kathleen would free herself from the shop, and he would have to make some really tough decisions.

Jack leaned across and studied her hand, the skin pulled tight across the knuckles as she wrote in her neat compact script. She folded the forms to fit in the envelope, and licked the seal with the tip of her tongue.

"I've been approached about a position," she said, "at Pinehaven School, coming available next year."

"I see," he sighed.

"I couldn't accept a teaching job without this," she said, waving the letter she had just signed.

He moved closer, put an arm around her. "We'll make it work," he said, without a clue as to what that would entail.

*

While Kathleen's mood improved, Jack's plummeted. The shop lease was ready for renewal in the new year, but without Kathleen's help, he couldn't see it continuing. To do so would mean hiring an assistant which was a situation he didn't really fancy. This left him with only one viable option – to get out of the retailing business. He truly loved the shop and depot. Meeting people, having a chat, sharing a joke or two: that was his forté. He thought of the other enterprises he'd dabbled in and enjoyed over the years; sign-writer, tie-maker, emcee to name a few, but he'd have to be the employee this time around.

Organising supplies was what he was most experienced at; running his shops and the company stores in Trentham had proved that. Working for the armed forces must be worth something and he knew how to talk himself up, if the need arose. 'Gift of the gab', was how Kathleen put it. He was a hard worker, good with money, he liked people, didn't wish to be bored, and was after a role which would give him autonomy.

Jack folded the newspaper on the Jobs Vacant section, and opened the shutters on the bookstall. Until a position popped out at him, he still had the shops to keep going.

Counting the takings

Colin continued to help run the bookstall on Saturdays, while Jack was at the Treadwell Street shop. It was stock-taking time and vital that he stay on top that, regardless of what happened when, for there may be someone who'd take on the business as a going concern. He hadn't the heart to tell Joe he'd be gone soon, and just waved to him through the window instead of stopping for a chat. He would tell him this coming week.

"How did we do today, son?" Jack asked, tipping the coins from the till into the small canvas bags the bank supplied for the job.

"We've done okay. I've already totalled up." Colin said.

"I think you deserve a treat, young man," Jack said, lifting the lid to the icebox.

He popped the ledger and money in his bag, for every Saturday evening was spent going over the takings for depositing in the bank on Mondays.

Jack enjoyed sitting at the 'new' table after dinner, feet on the strut underneath, family banter floating in the air, his work books spread out all around him.

He looked up at the wallpapered wall. The last of the big inside jobs. He'd got hold of some anaglypta wallpaper with an embossed leaf pattern through an old army mate. Cream it was – at first. But he had since painted it the same soft grey as he used on the kitchen walls. It had a sheen, showed off the pattern well. It looked great; tickled him no end.

"Still admiring your handiwork?" Kathleen asked good humouredly. She handed the last dish to James to dry and wiped the bench. Jack chuckled. James may as well have been asked to clean the toilet the fuss he put up. She was attempting to get all the children to help with household jobs. Looking ahead, like he was, probably.

"Oh, go listen to your programme," she told James, "you've not missed any you know."

Jack reached out as James ran past, but missed him. "It's good that you're helping your mother," he said.

While *'Life with Dexter'* burbled on in the background, Jack adjusted his armbands, and his pencil. Something wasn't adding up for today. It hadn't added up last Saturday either, nor the one previous, when he thought back. Or was it that he was so damned dog-tired when he did the accounts? But he could see now that the amounts had escalated. He flicked back through the ledger for the days Colin worked. Oh shit! The biggest losses correlated with those days; every one of them. Colin, Colin, Colin. He pushed his hair back, lit a cigarette and added the amounts one last time. "I need you to go over these Kathleen; something's amiss."

She took the ledger and looked the figures over. "You weren't wrong. The amounts just don't tally." She got up then and made tea, leaving him to fret on his own. Ah, it had given him indigestion.

This was going to be tricky. He'd have to ask Colin outright. He groaned. Confrontation wasn't his middle name. After the radio programme ended, Jack waited until James had gone to his room, went over to Colin and whispered, "I need to talk to you, in private." Jack kept his voice low when he questioned him. Colin's cheeks reddened.

"Dad. I check and double-check everything that comes in and goes out. You taught me that."

"Okay. Okay."

Jack saw how Colin wrote down the product sold, the money given and what he handed back. Colin also knew he'd be caught out if he'd done something so dumb. The boy was calm now, maybe weighing the implications of what his father was saying. "So, Colin...is there anything, anything at all you can think of? Do you think you might have forgotten to slip the nub when you've gone to the toilet? Something like that?"

"Mr Franks watches the shop when I need to use the toilet." Jack felt like throwing up. Larry Franks was the Station Master and Jack's friend; his whole family knew him. They visited his house to see the family's pianola, fascinated by keys and pedals needing no human hand. Please not let it be his mate who was fiddling the till.

"He said you asked him to help me."

"Can you remember when this began?"

"Not sure." Poor kid looked like he'd bawl any minute. "Maybe when the house was finished."

"Okay, son, tell you what. You are going to help me set a trap."

"Anything, Dad."

"Yes, well, I know how skilled you are at such things."

A stakeout

The following week, Jack had Colin open up the bookstall, parked his car on the opposite side of the station from his usual spot and approached the platform from the west. In a rough disguise of a hat, glasses and his old gabardine coat, he positioned himself in a seat-well, so he could see both the office and the bookstall when he leaned forward a little. The wind whipped cold on his neck with each movement. Larry Franks soon left his room, waved off the southbound train, and walked to the north end of the station where Jack lost sight of him for a bit. Ah, he'd come right around. There he was, at the bookstall, and in matter of minutes he was in and Colin was out, signalling to his father. Jack ran, reached the door and gingerly tried the handle. The bugger had slipped the lock. Crouching down he approached the front, and unfolded himself when he reached the opening.

"Looking for something?" he said, to the top of Larry's head, and he might have laughed if he wasn't the sucker in the story. But Larry Franks was clearly more experienced in covering his tracks, for he looked up and said, "Oh, hullo Jack, just covering the stall for Colin," and pulled on his cap.

"Just the once, is it?"

"Well. Poor kid needs to have a break, you know?"

"You know what, mate, I don't believe a word that's dribbling out of your mouth."

Jack darted around to the side of the stall, just as Colin reappeared, and Larry opened the door.

He and Colin, stood in front of the man, who tugged the peak of his cap. He had the nerve to smile, the cheeky sod. "Jack, you've got it all wrong. I'm telling you."

"And I'm telling you, Larry Franks, that this isn't the end of it by any stretch of the imagination."

Jack and Colin watched the station master return to his office, before entering their bookstall. They closed the shutters, gathered the ledger, the cash, and left, double-locking the door behind them.

Jack reversed the V8 from the parking lot and headed north. "I want you to know, Colin, that I believe what you've told me, about the takings and Larry Franks involvement."

"So, what will you do?"

"I'll go over the books for today – and all the days that Larry Franks supposedly helped you." Though he planned to examine them more.

"Then what?"

"First things first." Jack leaned across and patted Colin's knee. "You'll have to be a bit brave I'm guessing. Can you do that for me?"

*

After all the children had gone to their rooms Kathleen and Jack sat at the table with the bookstall ledger and the day's cash. "I should have made the bastard empty his pockets," Jack said. "What you did was right, Jack," Kathleen said. "Let's let the authorities deal with this."

"By 'authorities' I expect you mean the police."

"I certainly do." When Kathleen went to make the usual pot of tea, Jack lit another cigarette, coughing badly as he did, then sat with his head in his hands. "You're right, of course. Who knows how many other suckers he's taken advantage of."

"Who knows? But this is about us, Jack. It's our son and livelihood he's messing with."

He reached for the tin of Hardy's remedy from the cupboard.

"Indigestion again?"

"Not surprising with all this going on." But the powder seemed to help. One dessertspoonful dissolved in water at night.

Jack allowed himself a short break on Sunday, with the kids going about their different activities and Kathleen and he tidying up around the property. Late afternoon, he sat at the table and went through the books a page at a time. Come Monday morning he drove to Lower Hutt and parked outside the police station.

Quite how he was going to deal with the bookstall from here on in was a problem he'd tackle later.

Balls in the air

There were other things to examine as well as the stall's takings newspapers for example. Jack poured through the Jobs Vacant pages. There had been one he'd spotted before all this crap started; an office position at Certified Concrete in the Hutt. He'd not given it a second thought back then, hoping for something more illuminating to hit him between the eyes, but this week had changed his perspective. Oddly, he was buoyed a little, not by the back-stabbing friend of course, but the opportunity the thieving episode had presented. He no longer loved the bookstall as he once had, and the leaving of it, though painful, wouldn't seem so bad if he found himself a decent paying job to step into. The police were proceeding with charges, and a court case would ensue, meaning a lawyer and a good deal more money than he currently had access to. And not being cut from the same cloth as Larry Franks, he wouldn't be helping himself to someone else's pay packet.

He ripped the ad out of the paper and called "Kathleen, could you take a look at this?"

"You've nothing to lose by applying," she said, and almost as an afterthought, "I could help with the cover letter if you like."

*

The court case was painful, with Franks' lawyer pointing the finger at Colin, and the police not finding enough incriminating evidence to prosecute the stationmaster with more than the one crime; the day Colin and Jack had nabbed him. While the trial ran, Jack had James help out some days, as Colin no longer wished to. Couldn't blame him, really, but thanks to an odd turn of events, things were a little better at the station. Larry Franks' bosses had sat through the trial, and sent Old Scumbag packing to Wellington headquarters. A replacement was found for the Naenae office; a bonus, Jack felt, given the circumstances.

Before picking James up from an away game in Woburn one weekend, he dropped in to see Joe Wong. He left with a bag of rotting pumpkins.

"They stink," James said, as Jack sat the bag between them.

"Perfect for the job I've got in mind."

Jack drove up the Western Hutt Road past the Naenae shops, turned a corner and stopped under a large bottle-brush tree. "I know where we are," James said, pointing. "That's Larry Franks' place."

"Indeed, it is. And son, there's something I'd like you to do." Jack nudged the bag towards him. "Run fast, and empty the bag on the back porch."

"Dad."

"Please. For me."

And so, James did. Jack leaned over holding open the door, and as soon as James came back and hit the seat, Jack released the brake. "This is between us, okay?" he said, pushing hard on the accelerator.

But Jack couldn't resist telling his wife about his act of revenge, although he thought it more stupid than spectacular in the retelling. "But after what he did to you," Kathleen said, "he deserved a full dunny can dumped on his steps."

Life goes on

Since Kathleen and Jack had begun new jobs, the world seemed to turn faster. Kathleen was a different woman since returning to the classroom. She was happy. Jack could see that. A short bus ride to Pinehaven was nothing compared to train rides to the shop. Plus, she was home soon after their kids.

Colin was now at high school and James preparing for his entry into that domain, except, at Kathleen's insistence he wasn't to be following his brother to the co-educational secular school in Wallaceville, but attending St. Patrick's the Catholic boys' school just the other side of the railway.

"You've seen his talent," she said, before the choice had been finalised. "With his drawing and sports' skills, St. Pat's has more to offer."

Kathleen at Pinehaven School.

"James isn't Colin," Jack said. "There's no reason he wouldn't do well at the same school. They have sports and art at Heretaunga College, don't they? And why would you wish him to be at a Catholic school anyway?"

"The boys can't stand each other, is one reason," Kathleen said. She was right about that. Separating them might be a good thing. He had a sudden vision of his sons laying into each other at break, students cheering from the side-lines, teachers running to separate them.

Together they visited Kathleen's favoured school, and a few weeks later, James was the proud owner of a school uniform quite different from his brother's; navy blue shorts and socks, with two bands of light blue at the top. There was also a navy-blue cap, with one light stripe and a St. Pats monogram in the middle of the crown. "Very smart," said his mother.

Impressing the McPhee clan

The first term had barely begun when Colin arrived home one afternoon, opened his bag, pulled out a chanter and blew hard. He pressed his fingertips against certain holes and blew again, this time moving his fingers deftly up and down.

"What's the racket?" James asked, hurling his bag in the door.

Colin pulled a face. Poked out his tongue. "I'm learning the bagpipes," he said. "This is what you use to start."

"You're what?" his mother said, just in from work.

"I'm learning the bagpipes."

"And I suppose that you're very good at them?"

"I am, Mum; really good. Mr Andrews said so." Colin was still playing piano, had even talked of forming a group. She could see that music was his passion; but bagpipes?

Jack, who guessed he had some Scottish ancestry, thought the notion fun, and Colin added bagpipe-playing to his bulging list of musical accomplishments. Next, came the bagpipes themselves, carried home in a special case on an autumn afternoon and opened up for the family to see, as if it was treasure he was carrying.

In detail, Colin took everyone through the basics of looking after the pipes and bag. "I have to buy treacle," he told his mother, and proceeded to inform all, of how the warmed and diluted syrup must be sluiced through the bags for cleaning. He told them of a whole lot of other stuff too, which only Jack and Kathleen attended to. His siblings were rather revolted by this bagpipe cleaning process and had long since scarpered off.

Colin, however, excelled at the pipes while his academic prowess floundered. If it hadn't been for his teacher calling one night, Kathleen may very well have taken the bagpipes, case and all, and tossed them in the dump. The strength of the teacher's message was, he was 'rather hoping' that they would allow their son to join the Wellington Water-siders' Pipe band, where he and his sons were active members. "But why don't you come to the school gala next weekend and hear your son play?"

"Thank you for your call, Mr Andrews, for both your offers," Kathleen answered, thinking it was tough enough with James and all his sports. Boots for this, a bat for that; and running him around to his 'away' matches. Why couldn't Colin just stick with piano?

*

The rest of the McPhee clan watched the college band strut up and down on the grassy field; pipes piping, cheeks plumped. Children, including the girls, jigged up and down on the side-lines.

"This could be good for him physically," Kathleen said. "The marching I mean, Jack."

"You have to agree he's good." The band stopped marching, the dancers stopped dancing and the family watched their son. Hot. Smiling. And they smiled back.

"What did you think?" he asked coming closer, sweat flicking off his forehead.

"You were terrific," Kathleen said.

*

"Thank goodness I'm bringing in a decent wage," she said the following week, "as you know what the next request is from our Colin, soon-to-be piper in a Wellington pipe band, don't you?"

"No."

"Jack. What do Scotsmen wear when they play the pipes?"

"Oh Jeez, a kilt ... and spats and a sporran."

They avoided debt by buying garments second-hand from the club rooms. "Notice the pile of tartan?" Jack said. "Hope this uniform is not headed for the same fate." And they'd not yet accounted for the cap, plaids and brooches.

Fun for some

Colin continued to play the bagpipes, the girls joined Mrs Bennett's choir, and Sophia started piano lessons with the same teacher. Choir was fun. James went too, and they all loved singing in the group. But when it came to Sophia's piano lessons, she found the opposite was true. Mrs Bennett wasn't Mr Atkins; the only teacher she'd ever wanted, but he had retired from teaching the previous year and there was nothing she could do about that. Each Thursday she had to endure long theory lessons which dampened her joy of piano. After weeks of faking illness on Thursday mornings, Sophia got her way and piano was ticked off her list.

Weekends were fun though, as she got to bake, though Beverly, as always, had to join in. Kathleen, never keen on playing the conventional mother or housewife, was happy to let the girls develop their budding cooking skills. Skills learned at school. 'Manual' education was introduced in Forms One and Two, and since Sophia was now among the senior girls, she attended weekly cooking classes. At home they were allowed to choose what they wanted to cook, which usually meant going shopping for ingredients. But first they read through the biscuit list in the Edmonds Cookery Book.

"Let's make gingernuts," Bev said. "Like the ones Mrs Jones makes."

"Okay. You read the ingredients and I'll check we've got them."

"Butter. Golden syrup. And something with a long name."

"Bicarbonate of soda."

"Brown sugar. Flour. Salt. And ground ginger."

They had everything except ground ginger. They laid it all on the table, including the bowl, spoons and tray, got money from their mother and raced off to the shops for the missing ingredient.

Sophia set the oven to 350 degrees, handing over the tray-greasing job to Beverly. "Ooh," she said, wriggling sticky fingers at her sister. Sophia was too busy to look as she was creaming the butter. It took ages to go all smooth as she'd learned in class, but it wouldn't go pale like it usually did because of the golden syrup. The soda bit was fiddly as it had to be dissolved in hot water. But she did it. Bev helped roll the balls of dough. Sophia pushed the balls down with the back of a fork rubbed in flour and placed the tray in the oven. Fifteen minutes was all it took before she pulled them out, baked golden and smelling delicious.

"They look beautiful," Beverly said, "but we are very grubby." Sophia looked at her sister's apron smeared with dough and flour. "That's what real cooks look like," she said, untying her own and shaking it out the window. "But dishes now, little sister, before Mum comes in and sees the mess in her kitchen."

*

Kathleen's cousin Joan, made a rare visit that afternoon, bringing along her daughter Dawn. The girl looked uncomfortable; shoulders hunched, and no smile for any of them. Probably got that from her mother, Jack thought. Joan was a moaner, and when she started a tirade on her husband's shortcomings, he excused himself, saying the potatoes needed digging in. He picked up a spade from the lean-to, one of the few things left standing in the house overhaul, and had begun turning the soil when he heard the girls out on the concrete in front. His two were sitting on the ground, watching Dawn buckle the straps on her roller skates.

"Since when could you skate?" James asked, from the top of the steps. Sophia stopped shunting along the concrete; stared him out. "Since Dawn let me try them." He looked the girl up and down, "Oh, hullo," he said, and kept walking, his sports' bag bumping against his leg.

"Don't worry about him," Sophia said.

"He's a boy, so why should I?" was the answer and the girls skated in turns around the yard until their mother called them in.

"The girls baked these," Kathleen said to Joan, passing around the fresh biscuits. "Mm tasty," she said, and everyone else who tasted them. Sophia felt very proud of their efforts.

*

"Has anyone seen the syrup tin I left in the top cupboard?" Colin asked later that day. Sophia heard him. But he couldn't mean the golden syrup tin. That was just for baking.

"I put it there specially; it's for cleaning my bagpipes."

"But you told us you used treacle."

"Yes. That's in the big tin out back. But what I already used to sluice out the bag, I put in a golden syrup tin."

Sophia stared at him. "I took it," she said.

"What for?"

"Biscuits," she said, her bottom lip wobbling. "And we ate them."

Colin started laughing, but stopped when Jack grabbed his shoulder. "They were pretty good biscuits" he said, his shoulders shaking. "But I suggest Colin, that you keep your delightful bagpipe mixture well away from the kitchen in future."

It did take a while for Sophia to recover from the 'biscuit scenario' but didn't stop her from her baking. Jack did have to stop himself however, from referring to Colin and his bagpipes for a while, despite it being such a good story.

It's hard to believe the behaviour of some

It was just before the August holidays when Kathleen made an announcement. Not so unusual in itself, but when she stated, "I would like to go down and help out when Maxine's in the home with the new baby," Jack wasn't sure how to react. Maxine and Graham had not only moved since he'd last visited Oamaru, but they had taken on a business managing the Queens Hotel, around the corner from the cottage in Eden Street. Maxine was due with baby number two in a matter of weeks and his wife actually wished to go down there. "What would you do?" he asked, his tongue sticking on his lips.

"Manage the desk. Book guests, I imagine."

He honestly didn't know how he felt: thrilled on the one hand that Kathleen was reaching out to Maxine, but praying on the other, that this was a genuine gesture.

It was a cold, overcast day when he drove Kathleen to the Wellington Inter-Island Ferry. "Yes, Jack, I'll phone you," she said, taking her suitcase, receiving his kiss. The girls chose not to come. Still harbouring the hurt, he imagined.

"Maxine's had a baby boy," he told his children, coming off the phone. "They're calling him John."

"I'll write to Maxine," Sophia said. "No, I've got a better idea. Bev and I will make a card."

"Each," her sister said.

While the girls were busy cutting card and drawing, Jack got to thinking, and up popped a rather terrific idea. A couple of phone calls and the plan was in action, to enable his going to Oamaru and see his new grandchild first hand. Lucky it was the school holidays.

The girls would stay next door and the boys remain home, but with Carole and Bill's supervision. His boss was fine about taking leave without pay, and even wished him a good trip. The only thing left, was to get there.

It seemed a good idea at the time

As the train rolled into Oamaru, Jack rehearsed his lines. He pulled on the tartan cap, arranged the striped scarf around the shoulders of his borrowed black coat and stepped off the train. Boy, was it cold! Fog was clinging to the ground. A milk truck clanked by as he walked down Stuart Street, his bare hands freezing. Not far he thought, ducking into a shop doorway to don the horn-rimmed glasses he'd brought especially for this moment. He lit a smoke, checked his outfit in the window, puffed for a bit then ground the butt out with his heel. He coughed. And again. Right. In you go, Jack.

He pulled the cap low over his forehead and approached the desk. Kathleen had on her blue woollen skirt and cardigan, and looked particularly lovely. Her hair was almost grey now, but still thick and wavy. "May I help you?" she asked.

"Do you have a room available?"

"Just the one night?"

"Two please." She looked up, studied him for a second or two, picked up a pen and said, "Name?"

"Mr Dennis Perkins."

She turned the register around to face him and laid the pen down.

"Your address, please."

Jack wrote out their home address, and spun the book to face Kathleen. She glanced down then stood upright, shoulders back, chin high. Jack took off the glasses then the cap. Smiled at his wife. Oh dear. Her neck was flushed. She pulled the blue cardigan tight across her chest and crossed her arms.

"You may think this is hilarious, Jack McPhee, but I can assure you that I certainly don't."

"Come on, Kathleen, it's just a bit of fun. Come on! Kathleen." The door behind her opened. Graham.

"Jack, what are you doing here?"

"You may well ask," Kathleen said. "Thought he'd play a stupid trick on me."

Jack laid his hand on the register. "Well, do I have a room, or not Mrs McPhee?"

"Of course, he does," Graham said, leaning across the desk to shake Jack's hand.

*

Kathleen remained frosty until the following morning, when her mood cleared like the weather, although a crisp breeze blew in from the sea. They walked with Pearl between them to the nursing home to visit mother and baby, lifting the wee girl in the air every few strides.

Jack picked Pearl up to look through the window. Maxine was sitting up in bed holding the baby. "Mummy," Pearl called. Maxine looked up, saw Jack and started to cry.

"Tears of joy I hope," he said, bending over to kiss her and baby John, against the tuft of soft fair hair on his crown.

"It's such a surprise," she said, shuffling over so Pearl could sit beside her. Jack held the baby's tiny fingers. "It seems so long since ours were this tiny."

Kathleen handed Maxine the yellow roses they'd bought from the corner store.

"You are very good at keeping secrets," Maxine said.

"You'll find your father's even better," she said.

By the time Jack was to leave, Kathleen appeared to have forgiven him. Maxine would be coming home during the week, and he would have Kathleen back the weekend after. As hard as it was to say goodbye to his South Island family, he couldn't wait to get back to the North Island lot. All things considered; he was a damned lucky chap.

Better relationships for a while

Jack went to watch James play cricket as often as he could, now that he had risen to the grand ranks of 1st Eleven. He enjoyed sitting with the priests on the green, yelling out the odd 'Howzat!' and waiting for his son to bowl. James was crazy about bowling and always made a meal of it. The sizing up of the pitch. Maybe his height helped there? The ball rubbing down the strides, and the one-two-step leaning forward, with the arm up and …over.

He watched the game for a while then drove to Maidstone Park. He'd taken up tennis again, much to Kathleen's delight. Dave Vickers, his old army mate was the one who enticed him back and they often played doubles when called upon. Singles was his preference however, having more of the grass court to run around on, and the opportunity to improve his rusty skills.

His being at the tennis club worked pretty well for the whole family; giving Kathleen time to attend the girls' ballet classes, or just have time to herself. She appeared more settled, happier with her lot, and was definitely pleased that he was pounding the tennis courts again. Not that he'd seen a diminishment of his waistline for all the sweat expended, although his serve was definitely benefitting.

Then Colin added to his list of interests, thanks to New Zealand's compulsory Military Training programme in schools. He already liked marching, and playing the pipes, but neither parent imagined he'd take to rifles the way that he did and started pestering to have one of his own.

"I am not stupid," he announced one Friday night after regaling them with his impeccable knowledge of firearms. "I know the danger. But I'm talking shooting targets, and pests, not people."

Jack sighed. "You are only fifteen. If you're just as interested six months from now, we'll do more talking then."

Colin looked at his father, a quizzical look on his face. "What about my having a car?"

"Oh, Jeez."

"I'll get my licence first. Like you said I could."

"I did?"

"Yes, Dad. My memory's awfully good."

Jack went to swipe him and missed. Colin reached for a kitchen chair and swung it out from the table. "Here, you might need this to stand on."

"Cheeky ratbag," Jack said and laughed, for his son was close on six feet tall.

"About the licence?"

"Just go and get it over with."

*

And with Kathleen too, things were improving, and all because of cousin Bernie's wife. Since moving to Lower Hutt, they visited often, and a friendship developed between the women. Miriam liked being out and about, meeting people, seeking new projects. Kathleen was one of them, or, that's how Jack saw it; the way she took Kathleen under her wing, introducing her to other women; suggesting she change her hair, buy a new lipstick, or a dress or two. But it was good to see his wife enjoying herself, although there was the odd remark of Miriam being a bit 'pushy'. Kathleen certainly needed a new friend. And he did too, if he was honest with himself. Moira and Tommy had taken the family to live in Hawkes Bay; a work promotion Tommy had said, and another state house to accommodate them. And that was the end of fishing trips in the Clinker.

"Sorry, I wasn't listening," Jack said.

"We've been invited to go ballroom dancing, with Miriam and Bernie."

"Interesting."

"It's at a friend of Miriam's place," she explained. "They have a small dance hall at the back of their house."

Now that was something, he thought. Novel idea.

"Well, do you want to?"

"Bit out of practice, aren't we?"

"Easily fixed, Jack." She walked over to the pine cabinet, which housed the turntable, and popped a record on. They waltzed around the limited space, knocking into the couch and wall divider once or twice when they attempted a dip or a twirl.

"Bit tricky on the carpet," Jack said, "but that was nice."

"So again?"

"As you wish, Your Highness."

Kathleen laughed, re-positioning her hand on Jack's shoulder and took his lead. "We were good," he said, when the music stopped.

Jack caught hold of Kathleen's hand, and brought it to his lips. "Thank you, my dear," he said, bowing with a flourish.

They followed Miriam and Bernie along the side of the house to the cleverly designed room, which Martha and Stan Barker had reconfigured as a dance hall. Immediately his eyes feasted on the glossy wooden floor; Jack wanted a matching hall for himself. Music wafted from speakers mounted high on the wall, coloured lights were strung underneath them. A turntable stood in one corner. A discreet contributions box in another.

"What do you think, Jack?"

"That it's ingenious."

From that first evening, Jack and Kathleen went to every Saturday 'soiree' they could manage, especially since items of music, singing and other routines were also part of the evening, plus a supper which attendees helped supply.

"Why don't you prepare an item, Jack?" Miriam asked one night while sitting out for the two-step. "Kathleen tells me you have a nice tenor voice."

He looked at Kathleen leaning back as Bernie swirled her around. She looked good in her teal dress. Danced well. Always did.

"Well, I enjoy singing, that's for sure."

"So, can Martha put you down for next week?"

Jack was in his element, singing his favourite songs. Kathleen accompanied him on the piano when appropriate. Yes, they got *Where'er you walk*, and a unique rendition of Nelson Eddy's *Trees*, where he felt it necessary to drop his voice to match that singer's baritone.

Kathleen and Jack's dancing improved over the weeks and they both agreed that a turn or two around a dance floor improved ones' constitution. "What about disposition?" Jack asked. "Well, there might be some of that too," Kathleen said, placing a kiss square on his lips.

They usually took the girls with them on these nights, although they sometimes allowed them a trip to the movies at the Woburn picture theatre, as long as they walked to the hall afterwards. Jack and Kathleen felt the boys old enough to manage on their own for these evenings, and hoped their decision to encourage independence in their sons would not see them regretting their decision.

*

James had discovered girls, and spent a good deal of time preening in his bedroom mirror, applying Brylcreem and fashioning his hair into a duck's tail, as was the latest craze. This was something neither Jack nor Kathleen expected so early on in the piece, as they naively believed he had limited access to girls, attending a boys' school as he did. They hadn't reckoned on his friends' sisters, or cousins, or Friday nights spent at the youth club.

"We can't even blame the Catholic church," Jack said, for his son had joined the group the Anglican's ran.

"Table tennis is a great cover you have to admit." Jack smiled, remembering his own popularity with girls when he was the same age. Charm had been his lure and he could see that James had long picked up that attribute.

"As long as he sticks to table tennis, and not hankypanky."

"Ah, come on, Kathleen." He put an arm around her shoulders and squeezed. 'He has to grow up, you know." Moira had warned her. Teenagers were a different breed.

More changes and possibilities

Jack had recently changed his job at Certified Concrete, and now worked for Murdoch's Foodstuffs in the city. He held the grand position of Travelling Salesperson with his territory encompassing the wider Wellington region. As a pale blue Austin A40 was now at his disposal, he sold the V8 to Joe for a song. It was a fair deal Jack felt for a trusted friend.

The new job suited Jack better, allowing him the autonomy he craved. He enjoyed going through to Waikanae, the furthest port of call, when he'd drive from the Hutt over Haywards Hill, and around the Pauatahanui Inlet. The road was narrow and unsealed with tight bends, but offered splendid views across the water, until it ducked through the hills and exited near coastal Plimmerton.

He had two weeks annual leave, and the planning for a summer holiday had begun. It was to be a season of travel it seemed, for Kathleen had been offered Aunt Agnes's cottage in Picton for the holidays, and Maxine had invited the family to come and stay at their crib in Gemmels Crossing, ten miles out from Oamaru.

"Well, they are both in the South Island, I guess," Kathleen said, after Jack proposed they drive down the island, with James and the girls. Visit Maxine, then carry on up to Picton. They could see Mount Cook. The lakes. She could feel herself catching her husband's enthusiasm. Jack would return to work once they arrived at Picton and she would remain with the children. By the sea. In summer. She was floating on her back, the sun on her face, kicking her feet slightly, the ripples emanating. Tranquillity; that would be nice.

And so, the family of five packed up the small car, ready for the long trip south. Colin was happy to make his own way to Picton for the last week of the holidays, as he'd procured a small job when Fifth Form ended as a telegram boy at Trentham Camp Post Office. It was the matter of Jack dropping him off at the wharf, and Colin boarding the ferry; a trip of around four hours to Picton, as opposed to the night they'd spend on the boat to Lyttleton.

Travelling by ferry was something they had all experienced, but this was the first time they had gone with a car. Colin would have loved this bit, Jack thought, as he sat in the ranks with other vehicles, awaiting the signal to move ahead. Jack rolled the window down, wiped his neck with a handkerchief, pleased he'd told the others to enter by foot. Gulls hovered. Sirens sounded. Chains clanked. And slowly the queue of cars moved forward, into the darkened belly of the boat. Once the cars' wheels were secured, he locked the car door and went to join the others. May the adventure begin, he thought, climbing to the higher deck.

*

Once off the boat in Lyttleton, they headed to a grocery store, purchasing supplies to make sandwiches to snack *en route*.

"They've got different drinks here, Dad," said James looking up and down the shelf.

"Quench, is nice," Jack said, "rather like Cola. But my favourite's Creaming Soda."

"It's not just drinks though, is it Jack? Now, what are those buns we call Sally Lunn's in the North Island?"

"Boston Buns. You know, I'd forgotten the differences."

"Well, calling a 'bach' a 'crib' is a pretty big one."

"True. The kids had thought that funny."

"Just what you're used to, I guess."

It was a long drive, and hot, but unusual things like watching for mirages shimmering on the hot seal amused James and the girls mostly slept.

"We're almost there," Jack said, as he drove across the Kakanui bridge, soon pulling in on the stretch of grass running in front of the cribs. It was a very green area and pleasantly cool. "I'll go and find their place," he said, and wandered off down the track. Kathleen marshalled the children out of the car and into the shade, fluffing out the front of her sundress to capture a very necessary breeze.

Maxine appeared in black togs, with a striped towel wrapped about her hips. Jack and Graham were next to appear, Jack with a blonde grandchild in each arm.

"We were just heading to the river," Maxine said. "Want to come?"

"Yes, please," said Sophia, running up to her big sister and hugging her hard. Maxine stroked her hair, and did the same to Beverly. "I can't believe how big you are now," and turning to their mother said, "they're a tribute to you, Kathleen."

191

It was a really nice welcome Jack thought, as he waded in the shallows with his trousers rolled up. Kathleen held her dress hem and did the same, while the children, all keen as mustard to go swimming, were soon in their togs and larking around. The littlies were a bit shy at first, but soon joined the others in the water, splashing and squealing.

Three days later they left the river, bumping over the unsealed road, winding the window up, as dust billowed up from the tyres. "Thank goodness for a main road," Kathleen said, winding the window down again. She fanned herself with a folded magazine, wishing she could return to the cool river spot.

They headed inland, driving alongside the Waitaki River. Jack pulled into a clearing. "Time for a photo, Kathleen?" She shrugged herself awake and looked out the window.

James was already outside. Apricot trees flanked the banks of the most beautiful turquoise-coloured water Kathleen had ever seen. "Girls, come and see. Here's something to pop in your memory banks."

The trip north was full of surprises like these, the family exclaiming at every new scene; the bronze of the hills against cobalt skies, old towns and museums they visited. It was a stinker of a day, however, and getting hotter. It was made worse by turning onto the unsealed road winding up the centre of the island. They had plenty of drinks to get them through, but the heat in the car was bringing on stupor. "We made it," Jack yelled, driving out of the dust, pulling up beside Lake Pukaki. They practically rolled off their seats, high-stepping to the lakes edge; yet again, that beautiful turquoise-coloured water.

Jack removed his cap and scooped it in the lake. "Daddy,"

Bev laughed, when he tipped the water over his head and stuck the hat back on.

"How unpleasant," his wife commented.

"I'm nothing if not inventive," he said, repeating the cap wetting action. Everyone waded in the lake, before sitting under a flimsy willow. Kathleen pulled out the sandwiches, and the 'I'm too hot' grizzling was over for the time being. Before leaving they viewed Mt Cook, reciting its height of 12349 feet that they learned like parrots in school. Kathleen was pleased that her children knew about regional geography, even if it meant rote learning to achieve it. "Mountain viewing's over, sorry," said Jack. "One last cool off and we're going." James grabbed his father's cap and scooped it full of water, chasing him up the bank.

"Here, Dad," he said, flipping water from the hat.

Slightly cooled, they climbed back in the A40, all with wet hankies to dab hot heads. Kathleen draped a hand towel around Jack's neck, and soon he started singing. *"There was an old lady who swallowed a fly, I don't know why she swallowed a fly"* ... and aiming for a bass, sang *"Perhaps she'll die."*

This was a cumulative song, which added a different creature each verse, and got faster, as it went along. The kids loved the 2nd verse, and he could almost hear their halted breaths, waiting in anticipation. *"There, was an old lady who swallowed a spider, which wriggled and jiggled and tickled inside her. She swallowed the spider to catch the fly, I don't why she swallowed the fly. Perhaps she'll die..."*

James knew all the verses and Jack let him continue leading. The silly song and the enjoyment it spread was worth a letter to

Burl Ives, the man who'd popularised the ditty. The singing and scenery made them forget the miles still to go.

Lucky for Jack that he was staying the night in Waikawa Bay before catching the Friday morning car ferry to Wellington. He had a weekend to rest before starting back at work, and delivering Colin to the south-going ferry.

Waikawa Bay

It was a mile or so into Picton proper, but the children didn't mind the walk and were quite uncomplaining about the heat, except at night when the sunburn bit, and Kathleen lathered them with Calamine lotion. The waterfront was the drawcard, offering a nice swimming spot, a talent quest and plenty of girls, which brightened James' spirit no end.

The days were balmy, and Kathleen rose late, which was something she never usually indulged in. They went to bed at dusk and rose at dawn, as Tilly lamps were the only form of light available. Being tall, Colin got the job of lighting the wicks, and settling the glass dome back in place once he got the right adjustment. The decorated china wash basin intrigued the children too, as did the large jug for water. Cold water only; though they all should be well used to that. Fortunately, there was a gas stove, though the kitchen was poky and the black cast iron pots hard to use. She'd develop muscles by the time she went home she thought, as she hefted a pan to the stove to poach eggs.

One morning, Kathleen sent the children to the beach under Colin's supervision, while she continued talking on the phone to their dad. She closed the gate, looking out to the clear sky and placid sea, and sauntered along listening to the gulls and boats shuffling in moorings. Soon her togs were sticking to her under the dress, and sand was getting in her sandals, but, with a mile still ahead of her, she wasn't about to run.

The waterfront was immaculate, with phoenix palms stepping down beside paved stairs to the sea. She had never been to England, but this is how she imagined seaside towns might look. Regal, and proper somehow. White ornate walls finished off the grassed areas. Neat and tidy, the opposite of any garden she'd known. She scanned the sea, cupping her eyes against the glare. One, two, three and four children. The girls were near the sand and the boys out further. Kicking off her sandals, she slid off her dress, and entered the water waving and calling, "Colin, you've got School C."

"What?"

"You've got School Certificate," she called louder. He moved towards her, grinning. She plunged in and swam closer. Splashed him as she stood. "Well done," she said.

"Did Dad tell you?"

"He phoned, just after you'd left."

"What did I get?"

"I only know that you passed."

The next evening Kathleen took a picnic down to the beach, as dear James was going to be entertaining the holiday makers, by singing at the Sound Shell. She hoped it wouldn't be the *Ying Tong* Song, as she'd heard enough of that to last a lifetime. Still, the other children wanted to cheer their brother on, so she would just have to lump it.

It was like a children's music recital, that went on, and on, with few truly talented types in the line-up. James' name was well down the list.

"Colin," she whispered, "I give you permission to shake me if I go to sleep."

"Really?"

"Make that a tap on my shoulder." Kathleen wondered if any decent songs were being written any more. The *Yellow Polka Dot Bikini*, I ask you? And *Alley Oop*? She could barely cope with Paula Anka's *I'm just a Lonely Boy, Lonely and Blue...* but not this boy's rendition. He couldn't be more than ten. The children were clapping. Now James' turn. She clapped for him. The Tom Dooley song. Simple lyrics. *Hang down your head Tom Dooley, hang down your head and cry ...* Oh no, she found herself singing along. And James did quite well. But ... dear, dear, dear, she wished he hadn't sung the *Stupid Cupid* song with the imposed '*Greasy Jim*' lyrics.

"Never mind," she told him, when the lovesick child won. "How about I get you all an ice-cream sundae?" It had been a good time, she reflected, looking at her children, all apparently happy. They would be returning home soon and back to school for everyone. A new one for Sophia. Childhood was over too soon for some.

More teenagers

For all that Kathleen wanted Sophia to attend Hutt Valley High School, supposedly for better art tuition, she didn't get her wish, and so, come February, her firstborn daughter joined Colin at

Heretaunga College. Sophia had done well in her senior years at primary school, largely due to Mr Howie's innovative teaching. He was a warm and encouraging person, and his input saw her improve socially and academically. Jack, always bright, had received a Dux medal when he finished Form Two. A gold Maltese cross with his name and 1928 inscribed on the back, was what he passed on to Sophia when she finished primary school, near the top of Form Two.

He wasn't sure how his daughter would take the transition to a much larger school, with no friends in her class, and subjects taught by different teachers in different rooms. He tried to assuage her misgivings that first morning, dropping her at the station; smart in a grey pinafore and white short-sleeved blouse, telling her how bonny she looked, and dropping in the odd platitude about her getting used to it.

Beverley by contrast, was rejoicing in her new status as a senior at the primary school, taking jaunts to the cooking lab as her big sister had done, being involved with lots of sport, taking after James, showing off her skills.

Then Kathleen applied for a permanent teaching position: Infant Mistress at Silverstream School. "It's alright, Beverly," she said, the day she got the job. "I'll be in the Primmer block, a rugby field separating us. You probably won't even know that I'm there."

"But I'll know, and so will my friends," she said.

"You're a big girl now, aren't you?"

"Yes."

"Well, grow up."

*

James was growing way too fast, height-wise and socially, always dashing off to an after-game event, or party, hogging the bathroom for long periods beforehand. Jack was passing through to the lean-to one evening when he smelt a familiar odour; *Old Spice* if he wasn't mistaken… The door was slightly ajar and Jack gave it a nudge. And sure enough, there was James smacking the stuff on his face like a pro; hoping to appeal to some girl or another no doubt.

"Since when did you have my permission to use my aftershave?" he said.

"Can I use your aftershave, Dad?"

"Very funny," he said. "Time you had your own, son." He pulled a fiver out of his pocket. "For some *Old Spice*, and your own razor," although he was damned sure his son wasn't ready to shave. 'Bum fluff' he'd call it.

"Did you ask where he was going?" Kathleen was heating up an instant dinner. Again.

"To Lower Hutt with what's-his-name… Tim, I think."

"Ah, he's one of those nice Marist boys. So polite."

Jack suspected that James had primed the group beforehand. Kathleen was a stickler for insisting on knowing who was whom, and wasn't opposed to letting others knowing her opinions if they didn't meet scrutiny. Jack had had only to examine his own teenage years to be a little more concerned about the groups' true intentions for the evening. However, he'd met them at rugby, quite liked them all, and would believe, for the meantime, that the respective parents were aware of the 'garage party.' He pulled the foil off his meal, of an indescribable stew and wondered what he'd done to deserve this rubbish.

"See you about ten," Colin said, sniffing at his father's dish.

"Where are you off to?"

"Stephen's place; going to see what he's like on the saxophone."

"Make a good addition to the band."

"That's the idea." Jack looked up at his son's mop of unruly hair. Was there anything the brothers had in common?

Keeping a promise

Colin scarcely looked in a mirror, unless it was attached to a car, and had talked of nothing else since getting his licence. Jack had intended to help his son look for a motor, but Colin evaded any parental input by announcing he'd found one. An Austin Seven, quite the copy of *Noddy's* car; painted red and yellow with a black trim. Of course, Colin had done a deal with the local garage, where he now worked after school and the owner wished to rid himself of his own son's flight of fancy. Although, before it came to rest outside their house, Jack insisted he look the car over. Take it for a run.

"It seems in pretty good nick," he told Kathleen, who held a more sceptical view of her son's latest preoccupation. But knowing nothing about cars inner workings, she took Jack's word on the matter and in due course *Noddy*, the newly-dubbed vehicle, came to sit in their yard.

Colin treated it as if it were a Rolls Royce, rubbing and buffing until it was gleaming. "I can take myself to bagpipe practice now," he told his mother. Heaven help us all, she thought, looking at the Austin, thinking it resembled an overgrown pedal car. But

Colin drove himself and his mates all over the place like a young prince, flattered by the attention his unique vehicle brought him. Kathleen breathed a bit easier as the months went on, as her son appeared quite sound as a driver. They had even driven in tandem over the Rimutakas to Lake Ferry one weekend; the children taking short 'joyrides' in their brother's car.

It was a lovely day, Kathleen remembered, driving beside the lake, even stopping to pick mushrooms on the journey home. Maybe she'd have to admit, that this funny little car had some merit to it.

V8 and duck.

*

Then, one Saturday afternoon Colin arrived home just an hour after leaving for a pipe band function.

"You all right, son?" Jack said, looking up from his digging, to face a very glum-looking son.

"Yeah, I'm okay, but my car's not." And pointed to the road, where the red and yellow car sat, looking in a far worse state than his owner, with its roof caved in.

"Jeez, what happened?"

"I rolled it near Hayward's turnoff."

"You got into some loose shingle I'm guessing."

They both assessed the car, which seemed fine apart from the roof.

"Best thing is that Mr Sykes said the damage was 'just cosmetic'."

"And would cost a pretty penny to fix, I'll be bound."

"Unfortunately, yes."

"Right."

Kathleen was conveniently out, so they decided to play down the incident.

"We could say a duck dived into it; like the one that smashed into your windscreen that time?"

Jack sighed deeply. Yes, died on the spot it did, and Sophia, front seat passenger, bawled her eyes out when Jack suggested cooking it. What a waste having to bury the jolly thing; would have made a tasty treat. "Maybe not, Colin."

"Oh, and, a motorbike cop took my name. Might be around to see me."

"Looks like the truth shall out, don't you think?"

"I guess."

It was interesting listening to the retelling of the accident when the traffic offer came calling. Jack and Kathleen had always thought Colin dramatic, but never an actor. He could have shown Olivier a thing or two that night.

"That's right, officer. I got caught in the loose metal at the shoulder, and next thing, I'd flipped sideways."

The officer barely out of his teens, flicked back his hair, tucked his pen away and looked straight at Colin. "Luckily there was no one else involved," he said, "or we would have had to press charges."

"I promise to take more care in future, sir."

"And we'll see that he does, won't we, Jack?"

"That we will, Kathleen, that we will," he said, opening the door for the cop.

*

Jack was returning from tennis the following week, and could see Colin leaning over his car. The scene looked odd, not to mention the car, for as Jack got closer he could see all too clearly the roof being peeled back like the lid on a sardine tin.

He pulled up behind his son.

"I thought I'd save us some money," Colin said, waving a pair of tin snips.

"This takes the bloody cake, son..."

"But, Dad, I didn't want to ask you or Mum to pay for it. See, I've got some rubber tubing. If I slit in down the middle, it can go around the edge like this, then I'll have a pretty cool sports car."

Colin would always have an answer for everything no matter what the circumstances, and Jack felt that he had no choice but to help his over-imaginative son, even if it meant a swift trip to the wreckers.

"I've got some tough adhesive you can use, if you want?"

"I want," Colin said, "thanks, Dad."

"Your mother will be less enthusiastic about the transformation, I should imagine."

"She yelled a lot."

I'm sure she did, Jack thought, wondering if he should head in through the back door, when his wife appeared on the front porch, hands on hips, surveying the lie of the land.

She followed Jack inside, filled the kettle, and set the table for lunch. "You may want to sit down," she said, as he went past with the adhesive.

"There's more?"

"He's talking about getting a motorbike."

"That he's got a good deal for too I suppose?"

Kathleen nodded. "Kevin Jackson's got an old BSA he said he could have. Though it needs repairing.' Jack laughed. "I'll talk to him. Set him straight on a few things."

"What's with the glue?"

"Don't ask."

*

"Decided to leave him to it," he said, sitting across from his wife, helping himself to a corned-beef sandwich.

"I think we should look into a career path for him."

"A proper job, do you mean?"

"An apprenticeship; learning a trade. I think it would suit him."

"What about school?"

"I'm thinking after he sits University Entrance."

"What if he doesn't get it?"

"Come on Jack, this is Colin we're talking about."

He laughed, reached for his tin of Park Drive and rolled himself a smoke.

The year rolls on

At the end of the year Kathleen asked Sophia to help decorate her classroom. "Got to put those art skills to good use," she said. Sophia was just happy to be asked. She missed her old school, where teachers used to ask her to write out song sheets and decorate them, and to help slower readers in class. Her mother often pinned her students' art work and stories around the walls, but insisted that the blackboard was 'her domain', with an alphabet in perfect *ball and stick* script written in white chalk across the top.

"How about we do Father Christmas with his sleigh and reindeer along the bottom Mum?"

Kathleen handed her a box of coloured chalks. "Anything's fine with me."

Sophia always tried to do her best work for her mother and the drawing that day was no exception. "Good job," Kathleen said, admiring the jolly red and white man, and his prancing reindeer with crowns of fruiting holly.

"I couldn't fit all the reindeer on," Sophia said, "So that's why I just did half of one at the end, so it looked like more were following."

"That's smart. I like the holly, by the way."

Silverstream School Primer block

"I want to be an artist when I leave school, Mum."

"Goodness me, no. Art's no vocation. Teaching would be a far better option." Sophia looked around the room, where she had sat crossed-legged on the mat not so many years before, and sighed.

Different interests

In the new year Colin began an apprenticeship at Philips Electronics factory in Naenae. A relief to his parents, and probably his long-suffering teachers. How nice it was, not be in a constant state of worry, or alert, and to find that fiddling with bits for television sets was right up Colin's alley.

Jack's new job had many advantages that he was discovering too; time to himself, to listen to the car radio, or to sit and sketch the environment during his lunch-breaks. Along the road circling the inlet, there was a large degrading macrocarpa tree stump behind a sagging wire fence, which was where Jack parked and pulled out his art pad. He only had paper fit for oils, but it'd do for a quick conté crayon sketch. He held up his thumb for an idea of proportion, and made the first lines, and again, until he had a fair resemblance of the stump on the page. It had character, he reckoned, the bark dry and scarred from wind and sun.

This foray back to drawing promoted new interest for Jack, and he found himself looking for other subjects he might flourish his pens, pencils or brushes at. On his trips to Wellington he drove alongside the river, and he loved the part near Belmont where the river flowed silvery and sinuous, the willows on its banks and distant hills a mix of yellowy green. Wouldn't that make a nice painting, he thought. He could sit in the open and sketch the scene, and use oils, not watercolours, to create the rippling effect on the water. It would require more than a few minutes grabbed over lunch, however, and he began dreaming of trips on the weekend, where he might settle with his painting gear on the riverbank.

"You could come with me, you know?" he told Kathleen, as he prepared a board to take with him the following week.

"Marking, sorry."

"Can I come, Dad?"

"You got paper, pencils?" Sophia nodded. Kathleen was pleased to get Sophia out of her room, where she spent hours writing in her diary; no doubt about the skinny boy she'd seen her gawking at, when they were up town Friday night. Anything to take her away from that teenage nonsense.

That day at the river marked the renewal of Sophia's interest in drawing, and with Jack, all things to do with art. He said it was to encourage his daughter, when often it was to please himself, when he came home with new artbooks to study at the weekend. He was gaining quite a collection; random, though all interesting and informative, from the Tate Gallery Collection, periodicals about Van Gogh or Cezanne, and a wonderful book by Sir William Russell Flint. It was the last artist, who spent years in Spain drawing beautiful women, with clothes on and without, who held Jack's attention. The way Flint created form with conté and charcoal was nothing short of amazing.

Jack joined a Life Drawing class at the Hutt Art Society and found it the perfect fit: a place to meet other scribblers and extend his art skills. "What do you think, Kathleen?" he said after class one evening, holding out a charcoal sketch. The woman was reclining, back facing, and though his lines were chunky, he'd caught the pose well enough.

"It's modern. Unusual."

"I'll take that as praise." He held the picture against the anaglypta wallpaper. "It needs more texture, I think." And taking a stick of charcoal, rubbed it across the bottom of the work. He held the drawing at arm's length, tipped it sideways and back. The leaf pattern had come through nicely. "What do you think now?"

"Different."

"Whoo hoo," said James.

"It's just a backside, for crying out loud. A way of drawing form.'

"Sorry."

"What do you learn in art classes?"

Reclining nude.

"How to draw cubes, pyramids, and stuff. Where the light source comes from."

"Same light and shade principles," Jack said. "See here, where I've graded the tone around the leg."

"You've got homework, haven't you James?" Kathleen said, ushering him ahead of her, returning quickly, to suggest that Jack keep his nude drawing to himself.

Of course, he knew James was rather preoccupied with the fair sex, but surely simple drawings were not going to turn his head, as was Kathleen's intimation. Just as well he hadn't invited him to classes, but there was another he could.

Sophia went along to the class a number of times, and did very well overall. "You have a good eye for proportion," he told her, "quite different from your old man." Jack knew he wasn't that accurate, but it didn't worry him an inch. Colin wasn't too keen on the pastel portrait he'd done of him though. He had been looking at cubists and cubism, and rather liked the wonky work, as if it were cut up and realigned. Imaginative it was. Clever. Rather like his eldest son.

An addition to the family

Their neighbours' German Shepherd had a new litter, and guess who felt for sorry for the pup no one wanted? Kathleen. "It's been years since Prince died," she said, with some hesitation, knowing how Jack had loved the white Samoyed he'd had throughout his army days.

"And see how we all love him," Bev said, reaching into the make-shift bed to pat the puppy. "He's so gorgeous and fluffy." It was also true that the children were rather pet-deprived, since Kathleen insisted they give Whiffy the rabbit to a neighbour who kept several.

"He's going to grow huge," Jack said, "Just look at the size of those paws."

"We'll look after him, Mum," from James. "I can take him for walks."

"Me too – promise," from Sophia, and Colin. And despite Jack's mild misgivings about the German Shepherd and likely Labrador cross, he told Carole and Bill they'd take him.

Kathleen found an old suitcase, folded a blanket and carefully placed the puppy in. She covered him with some old nappies for extra comfort, and offered him warm milk. The children crowded around, each offering little gems of helpfulness. She thanked Colin for the best solution, when the puppy started whimpering, and he fetched the old alarm clock from the cupboard. "He'll be

Jack and Prince

missing his mother," he said, wound the clock, found a large sock to pop it in, and nestled it close to the puppy. Kathleen was the one, however, who sat with the poor wee thing, and settled him down several times through the night when he woke whimpering. She also named him Kingi.

"A special name for boys in Māori. A derivative of King," she explained; her interest piqued in things Māori since learning of a family connection.

Jack rather liked the continuation of the royal dog-naming and grew to love the rogue this king became. His ears, nose and tail were black, with the rest of his body a yellowy tan. He would sit on his haunches, head tilted, one ear up, one ear down, appealing to anyone who'd pat or feed him. The children were supposed to feed and walk him – keeping to a roster. And while he was small and cute, it worked, mostly.

Kingi grew however, to those rather large proportions which Jack had predicted, gaining muscle and strength really fast. The girls could no longer handle him on a lead, and Jack didn't need a crystal ball to see who'd be left with the exercising. He tied him up at night, letting him off when he rose in the morning. Kingi was always at the back door looking for food within minutes, until the morning he wasn't. Jack was about to send James to go looking for him, when he heard a noise on the front porch. No dog, but a pair of work socks and a half-pint bottle of cream.

"Kathleen, come and see what the dog's brought home."

She was grinning. "What do you want me to do?"

"I thought maybe someone should try find the owners."

"How do we know where he went?"

Jack heard the dog at the back door, took hold of his scruff, and attached him back on the long lead. He knocked on the boys' door. "Dog needs a feed."

"Bye kids," he called, "see you this arvo."

*

Kingi continued to bring home a miscellany of goods, from a baby's bib to a Dominion Post. Kathleen had felt it necessary to canvas the neighbourhood herself, and for the most part linked article with owner. They had always kept good relations with the neighbours, but as understanding as they appeared to be about the frisky filching dog, she sensed there'd be a limit to their patience.

Jack and Colin took turns driving Kingi and whichever family member wanted a swim to the river on the weekends. At least the dog could race around there to his heart's content. It was fun watching him leap across the stones to the water and appear coat dripping, to then shake himself vigorously on unsuspecting sunbathers.

Jack was returning home from the river one Saturday, the driver's window down, Kingi panting in his ear, when he heard bagpipes. They got louder. *Scotland the Brave*, he liked that one. Kingi, head hanging out the car window to catch the breeze began to howl and that's when Jack caught sight of Colin, standing a few feet in front of their porch, pipes in his arms, playing with his eyes closed. He left the dog in the car, and bounced down the steps past Colin, grabbed the dog's lead and returned to the car. "What's up, Dad?" Colin said, releasing the chanter.

"It seems Kingi's allergic to your pipes. Don't start up again, until I've got him inside, alright?"

"How come Colin's practising here?" Jack asked Kathleen, who was hunched over a pile of exercise books.

"A double booking of the usual hall. And competitions next weekend."

"The dog hates the bagpipes."

"Not just ours, Jack."

Colin resumed playing and Kingi resumed his howling. Jack could see why the German Shepherd had been referred to as a Wolf Dog. He walked around the section out onto the road, and oh yes indeed, barking resounded around the streets alright.

"Oh, hullo, Kay," he said.

"We're loving the concert," she said. Jack looked up Pempsey Street, where several neighbours were on the footpath with their children. Then Kingi howled again and he and Kay started laughing.

"I never thought *Scotland the Brave* could be this amusing," she said. Neither did Jack, but walked over to talk to Colin, who grumpily folded up his pipes. "We better not lose the competition next week," he said.

Unpredictable events

"I just can't believe you're going to high school," Jack said, kneeling down to tie Bev's shoe laces.

"I can do them."

"Indulge your old man. I may never tie your laces again."

"You're silly, Dad."

"*Gonna take a sentimental journey, gonna set my heart at ease, gonna take a sentimental journey, to renew old memories...*" he sang. "Now, give us a hug."

"I can walk her to the train."

"That's nice, James." He remembered how Bev had loved him walking her to kindergarten when James was just a kid. Ten years ago, that was and they were still good mates.

Sophia looked on at the newbie in her school uniform, wondering how long it would be before she let her socks droop, or turned her beret inside out. It wasn't hard to break the stupid uniform rules.

Kathleen waved them off, hoping that Beverly would not follow her sister's lead with her schooling. Sophia was almost top in 3rd Form to near bottom in the Fourth. Even with French, which she'd loved that first year and achieved so well, she was sliding backwards. Heavens knew what would happen with School Certificate exams at the end of the year.

James had sat the exam twice, through having too many interests. But he had passed, and credit to him for that. He surprised his parents by lapping up Military Training, although, unlike his brother, he preferred marching and giving orders than wishing to shoot vermin with a rifle.

"Have you considered an army career for him?" Father O'Connor asked Jack during cricket, one Saturday.

"God, no. Oh, sorry, Father, but why would you suggest that?"

"James is officer material I hear."

It was all a lark as far as he knew it. *'Boy's Own* stuff' as James had said. He hadn't imagined a different scenario. "Thanks for the head's up for the military for James, Father. Will have a think about it."

Fighting. War. He certainly hoped it wouldn't be his son's lot. Being on the periphery was bad enough.

And Beverly was thriving at secondary school. Having friends from primary school in her class may have helped at the start, but Jack suspected it was her forward, sporty nature which set her up – gave her confidence.

"Guess what?" she said, barely a week in the new school. "Our gymnastics team is going to perform for the Queen, and I'm in it."

"What?"

"I auditioned for a balance beam routine, and…they took me."

"That's terrific," Jack said. He'd seen her on the beam; the way she could balance, flip over and do other bendy body things. He had no doubt she was good. But before they could concentrate on this piece of excitement there was the matter of Colin and the television set.

Something to boast about

Colin had been beavering away for weeks as he put together his own television. He brought home transistors, resistors and capacitors in a shoe box, bribing the girls to help sort out the tangled mess. Each of the components was colour-coded and Colin figured a smart way to assemble them. He laid a piece of card on the floor, corrugations facing up, and with a diagram of the circuit board in front of them matched the tiny bits in their correlating positions on the card.

All this industry took Jack and Kathleen's mind off Sophia as they became fascinated with their son and what he was doing with the television paraphernalia. Especially when he began testing the tube. Once everything appeared to be connected correctly, Colin brought home an oscilloscope (on loan from the factory) to analyse the waveform. "Which means observing and testing the voltages and amplitude frequency over time," he announced.

"Right," Jack said, tutting in understanding. It might have been Russian he was hearing for all he knew.

Colin had constructed an aerial and he needed Jack's help to erect it on the roof. With James' help in holding the ladder and passing tools up to him, then on to Colin, slowly the unwieldy object was up. And Colin was down, attaching the garden hose to the tap and unwinding its coil.

"Can you stay there for a bit, Dad?" he said, dropping the hose on the ground.

"To do what?"

"I'm going to test the signal. I'll yell out when I need you to adjust the aerial."

"Jeez." Jack was finally relieved of his chore and went to see what had transpired in his absence. Colin was in front of the screen, ecstatic. What for, his father couldn't ascertain, as he clearly hadn't got a picture.

"See, Dad," he said, "That's the test pattern, which means I should be able to get an image."

"Tonight?"

"Maybe not. I'm going to check some things out first."

"And then?"

"Invite people around to watch it when it's going."

*

The moment to view the television had almost arrived. Jack helped move the oak side-table near the window, and placed the television on top, now cased in a simple cabinet Colin had acquired from his work. This meant more checking and re-checking of the TV, but Colin was determined to improve the shivering image on the screen. One novel idea was to hose the aerial intermittently, but be damned if Jack knew why. At intervals, Colin yelled 'start', 'stop' to his brother or sisters, who begrudgingly took turns holding the hose. James stormed in after his turn, hair dripping wet.

"I didn't ask you to take a shower," Colin said.

"What did your last slave die of?"

"Stop moaning," he said, "you'll be skiting soon about having the first television in the street." That seemed to appease James momentarily, who also had the job of telling neighbours they would be 'on air' Sunday night, and to come over if they wanted, about quarter to seven.

Kathleen got the girls to help her clear the dishes, and set the table with an assortment of bought biscuits on plates, including Colin's favourite malt meal wafers. She wiped the seats of the kitchen chairs and turned them to face the TV. "Give me a shout when someone comes," she said, "I'm going to clean up the bathroom."

There was knock after knock, as Jack ushered people in. When Kathleen returned to the lounge, every seat was taken. "Come in Kathleen," Jack said, laughing. "It seems we have ourselves a little party."

"Lovely to see you all," she said. Might have known the Reagans' wouldn't have missed this little treat.

"This could take a little while," Colin said, fiddling with knobs, until the form of the newsreader appeared on the screen. "Welcome, and good evening," he said, in a plummy accent, "I bring you... the news..."

There was clapping, and "Ooh, that's marvellous" from Kay. "What a clever boy," from another. "Shhh," from Kathleen. "It's about the Queen's visit."

"... Queen shall ... New Zealand ... the anniversary of ... succession ... throne..."

"Sorry about the interference," Colin said.

"It's fine lad," from Bert Taylor. "This is great."

"... Royal Yacht Britannia ... Bay... Islands Waitangi ... Celebrations ... sailing ... Auckland ... Tauranga to ... Napier on ... Wellington for ... opening ... Parliament ..."

"And seeing you at Athletic Park," Kathleen whispered to Beverly.

"... and ... Nelson ... the Queen ... shall ... Outward Bound ..."

The image was splitting and Colin sent off James to try the hosing technique. "I think that's it for tonight," he said, as the screen lost the image entirely. "It just needs a little more adjustment."

"Hey, no need to apologise son. You've done a great job," Jack said, patting him on the shoulder.

"I'll be back for more," Bert said.

"Lovely," Kathleen said. "Now how about a cup of tea?"

Unanticipated events

In another week Colin had ironed out the initial problems with the TV reception and it took some diplomacy to stop too many neighbours knocking on their door once the word got around.

"I bet we don't see the back of them, once they get their own," Jack said, after ushering a couple out.

"I hope you're right," Kathleen said, "or I'll never get my schoolwork completed."

A few days later Colin arrived home from work, shoved the door open and shouted, "Mum, Dad. Bet you can't guess what happened?"

"Get those boots out of here,' Kathleen yelled.

Colin emerged bootless, undoing the strap on his helmet. "Don't you want to know?"

"Sold *Noddy*?" Jack said.

"I've been offered a cadetship in Holland." His siblings appeared in the lounge and converged around Colin. Kathleen hurried over and kissed him. "Sorry for yelling."

"Mum," he complained, wiping his face.

"I'm so proud of you, Colin."

"Yeah, well."

"Likewise," said his father and thumped him on the back, while the others stood there grinning like clowns at an A & P show.

"That's pretty good," James said.

"Mm. Guess so." The girls sat either side of him. Bev offered him a toffee and Sophia a florin she'd found on the road on her way home from school.

"Beauty,' he said, "that'll get me an ice-cream or two."

While the fuss continued, Kathleen was thinking about money, money that Jack and she didn't have; and without knowing the particulars of this most surprising offer, she could imagine the cost.

Even with Jack's attempt to up the mortgage, her prophecies came true. In the end it was Jack who got rid of *Noddy*, to a motor-crazed kid at his work. He got a little for it and was fingering the notes in his pocket, wishing he didn't have to face his son that night.

Kathleen served a meal of grilled chops, gravy and roasted vegetables, a favourite of Colin's, with apple pie to follow. She had primed the others to scoot off when they'd finished. Tell him Kathleen. Get it over with, please.

"Well, the good news is, that your father sold the car."

"And we have something else for you." Jack handed over the second-hand leather jacket they had bought to soften the blow. Colin held it up. Examined the label. Eased it on.

"You look quite handsome," Kathleen said.

"I know I'm not going to Amsterdam," he said, sliding up the zip.

"Believe me, we wish it were different son."

"It's okay, Dad. Really."

Within minutes he was on his motorbike and showing off 'his leathers'.

"Colin took it well don't you think?" Kathleen said, closing the door.

"He seemed to."

"Cup of tea?"

"Might turn in, I think."

He went out the back to tie up the dog and stood, smoke in hand, looking up at the night sky seeking the Southern Cross. Kingi nuzzled his leg, and he reached to pat him.

"I'll have that tea after all, Kathleen," he called, "It might help my indigestion."

The Queen's visit

All schools had the day off for the Queen's visit and Kathleen took Sophia and James to Athletic Park where Jack was to meet them, having wangled a few hours off work to see the star performers, and the Queen, of course. He huddled with his family waiting for the royal walk about.

"It's great that Colin's playing today," he said to Sophia, who looked smart, in the tan skirt, and white top she'd made herself. He nudged her. "Nice shoes too," he said. White slip-ons with a heel, which she loved. He had taken the girls to Wellington as a treat and bought them new clothes. Sophia wore the coat immediately; a boost for her sagging morale.

James was pretending not to know them, and had hooked up with a friend. "There they are," someone yelled, "Here they come," and the crowd shoved forward, frantically waving little Union Jacks. The Queen. So young. Pretty. Waving back. And Prince Philip, rather a tall chap.

Here came the bands. The Military brass followed by the pipers. Wellington Water-siders were towards the rear. Jack removed his hat. Waved to his son. "C'mon, let's try and get closer." The bands marched in unison, drummers at the back lifting their arms high, clearly enjoying the occasion. Jack shuffled his way to the outside of the crowd to hunt down the gymnasts who were across the other side. The crowds were thinner, and the view unobstructed. With Kathleen and Sophia on each side, he watched Beverly do her routine. She walked that beam without a hitch, landing squarely from her off-loading flip. With a beautiful smile to finish. Kathleen took a photo.

The sun was shining, Kathleen was happy, and they were enjoying a day out. All because two of their brood were performing for the Queen. A bagpiper and a gymnast. Who would have thought? Now, if he could just locate James.

He found him leaning against the car, and could that be a cigarette butt by his shoe? "I did see you, but couldn't get to you," James said. "I watched Bev though."

"I hope so. Because here she comes."

Colin joined them on Petone beach for a meal of fish and chips. Jack and Kathleen stayed in the car with the doors open. Gulls screeched and swooped for chips the kids were dropping off the wall, until Kathleen shooed the birds away. "Come for a walk, Jack," she said, stepping onto the sand. "Ooh, lovey-dovey," Colin called, when Jack reached for her arm.

Seeking solutions

Sophia was so quiet that day at the park it worried Jack. She didn't appear jealous of her sister but he sensed her insecurity with the gap which had widened between them. At least she wanted to sew, and that was something positive. And she liked reading.

"She doesn't like sports, that's her trouble," Kathleen said. "Too much sitting on her backside."

Jack with Bev and Sophia.

"C'mon, she liked ballet, didn't she?"

"Mm."

"And tennis at primary school."

"Been a while."

Maybe he could take her to the club with him. That would mean a simple tennis dress, and sandshoes, but he was willing to provide those if it helped. Kathleen took Sophia into Hazelwoods department store in Upper Hutt and spent considerable time having Sophia try one white dress on after another. Nothing fitted well and that included the price. "Highway robbery," Kathleen said, "I'd be better off making you something." She found Sophia's communion dress at the back of a drawer, pleased to have made it two sizes bigger at the time, creating tucks in the sides as was her usual consideration. She unpicked the seams, removed the bits of cut cotton thread, and called to Sophia for a fitting. And although Sophia's mouth turned down at the try-on, she knew better than to challenge her mother and stood glumly as Kathleen pinned the hem to an appropriate length, using the school's three finger-width from the knee rule. The material was knobbly, the dress tight across her bust, but Sophia knew she'd 'just have to lump' it.

It was at tennis Jack discovered one source of his daughter's problems; for as soon as the games had finished at the club, up rolled a blue Humber that had seen better days. There were two boys plus the driver inside. One leaned out a window. "Oh, hullo, Russ," Sophia said casually. "Do you play tennis?"

Jack laughed to himself; a set-up if ever he'd seen one. "This is my Dad," she said, and the boy extended his hand. "Nice to meet you, Mr McPhee." The lad looked young, and no hoodlum, and his mates looked much the same. "Same," Jack said. "Russ, wasn't it?"

"We're off to the milk bar; alright if Sophia comes with us?"

"If you don't mind me tagging along?" Jack said.

Russ looked around at his mates. "Why not? Be nice to have someone to talk to."

"Did you like him, Dad?" Sophia asked, watching them drive off, tyres catching the gravel.

"I liked him and his friends, but it's not just my approval you'll need."

*

"I want to talk to you now," Kathleen said. "In our room Jack." Oops. Trouble with a capital Tee.

"I hope that I misheard what Sophia just told her friend Elizabeth," she said, pushing the door to.

"What is that?"

"That you took her to a milk bar with boys you just met."

"Oh, Kathleen. They're nice kids."

"Perfect specimens no doubt. But if that happens again ..."

"You'll what?"

"Stop Sophia going to tennis."

"For crying out loud ... oh, never mind."

Was there anything he could get right?

*

Sophia continued to worry him, and as the year went by it was clear that her teachers felt the same. When Jack attempted to learn why she thought the art curriculum 'uncreative' and 'boring', she said, "Dad, how would you like to make a tray with cane around the edges? It's like Occupational Therapy at the hospital."

"In spite of your views, and I'm saying this for your own sake, you must pull your socks up."

"But, Dad..."

"I have tried to help you Sophia, I really have. Help me here, won't you?" But Jack left that little chat feeling pretty low, wondering what it would take to turn their girl around.

Kathleen attended a parent teacher meeting later in the year, with the specific desire to have it out with the 5th Form Dean, who was also Sophia's English teacher.

"Do you know what she said, Jack?"

"No, Kathleen, but I'm sure you'll tell me."

"Miss Stuart said that she hoped Sophia would pass School Certificate ..."

"Don't we all."

"I haven't finished. The reason was, so she wouldn't have to put up with her in class."

"Great news."

"There's more."

"She and Elizabeth have clocked up a record number of detentions this term."

Jack breathed in deeply, exhaled. "This is Colin all over again."

"Worse. Sophia's not going to pass this exam."

"I'll put my thinking cap on; see what I can magic up."

"Anything Jack. Anything. I couldn't stand meeting that teacher again."

*

Monday, he left on his usual Wellington trip to Murdoch's and found his thoughts drifting to Sophia and how he and Kathleen could help the situation at school, when he accidentally shot past the Taranaki Street building and found himself on Wallace Street. Jack had often driven past the Wellington Polytechnic but taken little notice of it, but today was different. He remembered reading that the Polytech had been through changes and had set up a design school the previous year. He stopped the car, lit a cigarette, dwelling on a possibility, that maybe, just maybe, Sophia would take to such a school.

A diversion of a different kind

Jack pulled into the drive that night, a stabbing pain in his lower back. He rested against the seat and was woken with Kathleen tapping on the window. "What's wrong?" she asked, helping him out, and up the steps.

"Been doing too much, I expect."

"Is it the indigestion?"

"Don't think so. There's this pain," and he rucked his shirt up to locate the spot.

"You should see the doctor."

"Thinking along the same lines."

But Jack was in bed before he finally got to tell Kathleen about his day. Didn't have a chance with the children checking him out. They meant well with their "would you like your feet rubbed? or "how about a cup of tea?" "you're awfully pale Dad," to "you should lie down," routines.

"I spoke with the head of Wellington School of Design today," he said, hoisting himself up on his pillow.

"I'm listening."

"James Coe's his name, runs a full-time three-year course. The sort of subjects that just might appeal to Sophia. The first year has a bit of everything: general and life drawing, painting, print-making and design."

"It sounds interesting."

"She would have to present a portfolio of artwork for acceptance. Though Coe warned me that the roll is filling fast."

"Maybe we should both go and talk to him."

"Don't you think we should talk to Sophia first?"

"And we arrange this regardless of School Cert results?"

Jack leaned over and kissed Kathleen. "Regardless."

Toeing the line

Jack managed to paint a fairly grim picture of what Sophia might expect for the following year, if she didn't toe the line. "There are two options, basically. You produce enough sketches and paintings in the next two weeks for you to have any chance of getting into art school. If not – option two: in all likelihood you'll face another year with your least favourite teacher." He leaned in close. "Comprendo?"

He kept in the background as Sophia worked, who was sketching scenes out the window, around the house. Mm. Using both charcoal and pencil. Nice.

"Might be an idea to do something structural too," Kathleen suggested.

"Wouldn't they want to see designs, if it's a design school?"

"Thanks, James. Thanks, Mum. Now please leave me alone."

She didn't see her father follow them out and whisper, "Good suggestions; hope she's taken notice."

When Jack reviewed the artwork, he was thrilled with the variety Sophia had achieved; even writing the street address in well-spaced block lettering. "Nice rendering," he said.

"Do you like the painting?"

"You might have to sign it 'after' Cezanne. But I love it."

"Let's hope Mr Coe does too."

Jack glared at his wife. You bitch, he hoped he conveyed. Why couldn't she have said she liked it.

*

She was a little more reasonable when Jack came home clutching a pharmacy bag.

"What's wrong with you?"

"Yes, Dad, what's wrong with you?"

He took out a bottle of pills, read from the label. "Saccharin. No calorie sugar substitute."

"So?"

"Lose weight and see what happens basically."

"That's all?"

"And I've got Sacroiliac, the fancy name for a pain in the butt."

"Dad."

No use throwing more anxiety into the ring. When the doc had said the blood tests may be inconclusive.

Biding time

Six long weeks of waiting for results. For him, and his daughter.

He had pushed back the date for his follow-up doctor's check, so he could take Sophia to see her big sister. It seemed a perfect solution for a difficult time and keep Sophia out of her mother's hair for a while. Maxine and Graham were now living in Christchurch, and had themselves a nice wee house in the suburbs. Thankfully, Maxine was more than happy to have her sister stay. His plan suited Kathleen, with both boys occupied. James would be in Wellington most days; having scored a holiday job with Kirkaldie and Stains department store in downtown Lambton Quay.

"Don't worry about me, Dad," Bev said, "I'll be practising for the operetta."

"She'll be singing and dancing in Mikado, Jack."

"Clever, aren't you?" he said, doing a playful soft-shoe shuffle.

Bev walked over to the wall divider and did the splits up the wall. "Good Lord. Maybe you could join a circus."

"Dad!"

"Might be fun."

*

Then blow me down, James came home saying he was a likely candidate for Sandhurst or Duntroon military colleges and had been told by the priests to apply. "I'm not really sure why, although I did make Battalion Commander in the school's military training."

"Jeez, James. Here I was thinking you were just horsing around."

"Don't worry about it, Dad, because I'm not."

"Sandhurst, Jack. Can you imagine? Everyone knows about that academy; it's famous for producing top ranking officers."

230

"Duntroon is closer. The question is, do you wish to train as an army officer, son?"

"Nice to be asked. But no, I don't want to."

"It's such an opportunity James; surely you need time to think it over?"

"I have already Mum. I'd rather stay home and play rugby and cricket."

*

"It wouldn't have been fair on Colin," Jack said, "If we had decided James should go to England."

"He wouldn't have minded. You know Colin."

"Kathleen. That's not the point. Regardless of James not wanting to go. Have you forgotten why Colin couldn't go to Holland?"

"No, of course not."

"And you certainly can't have forgotten how your father died."

"I hear you," she said, her voice quiet.

"I'm sorry," he said, "I couldn't bear that to be our son's fate." He put his arms around her, held her for a while. "We can feel proud of his achievements though, can't we?"

"I guess so."

*

Jack left Sophia in Christchurch, returning home once he saw she was settled. It reminded him of that first trip south when she was nine and it was great to see the sisters slotting back into a relaxed relationship as if years had never parted them. "Don't fret," Maxine told him, "there's plenty she can do down here." Teaching Sophia to use the electric sewing machine was one bright idea and Sophia immediately searched Maxine's patterns for a dress she could wear. Jack was happy to care for Pearl and John, and played endless games of hide and seek on the square of back lawn, while the sisters shopped for material.

"It would be good if she could see her cousins while she's here," he suggested to Maxine, feeling guilty he'd not taken Sophia to visit the only first cousins she had. "Sophia is busy making a dress," he told Henry, when he had surprised him by knocking on his door that day, just a hop, step and a jump from his daughter's place.

"Be good for Maxine and Graham," he told Sophia before leaving; feeling the pang of separation from them all.

*

He arrived back home to find a small miracle had occurred: the preparation for the block wall was finished; the bank dugout. "It was your sons over the weekend," Kathleen said, "don't look so flabbergasted. Bert gave them a hand."

"I'll have to go away more often."

"To be honest, I was sick of waiting for my flower garden." They had both worked on the landscaping, nutting out some rough drawings, sorting out the structure of what should go where. They would have a block retaining wall, with a proper lawn fronting the footpath. Stepped-down flower boxes would be at one end of the wall. He had levelled the ground where the vegies had been, and sown a reasonable lawn, but had run out of steam when it came to the wall, leaving the blocks in a heap under the pittosporum.

"I offer you my humble apologies," he said, knowing he deserved the flak.

Jack had hoped for more painting before work beckoned, but

the block-laying had to be done in dry weather. Kathleen and the boys assisted him, to arrange the blocks in off-set rows, with Bert contributing his concreting skills to fit them. Jack insisted on stringing out a levelling line, as he wanted a professional finish. It was still hard work, even with helpers, but they got it done.

James and Colin helped to shovel the dug-out dirt into the boxes, and he and Kathleen added the topsoil. They were out there together brushing the excess dirt from the concrete, when Tommy and Moira walked down the steps with Milly their youngest in tow.

*

"Well I never," he said. "Things have certainly changed around here." Jack bashed the dirt off his hands and offered one to his old friend. Kathleen and Moira were hugging.

"What brings you to this neck of the woods?"

"Family issues."

"More like teenage ones," Moira said. "Shirley's in the car."

"Bring her in," said Jack. Shirley was pleased to see them both. But oh goodness, the hair, a fluffy blonde hive. Dyed, Kathleen swore afterwards. But it wasn't hair or clothing that bothered her parents, but the boy she'd got involved with who lived down the street.

"We caught her sneaking back in her bedroom window," Moira said, having sent Shirley outside with her sister. "It's getting us down. Mavis said she'd have her for a few days."

"Funny that," Jack said, and explained why Sophia was down south.

Kathleen pulled Jack aside, to suggest they could have Shirley to stay, after she'd seen Mavis, and organise her return to the bay.

Tommy and Moira thought it a great idea, as well as the sixteen-year-old daughter. Though why Kathleen wished to replace one difficult teen with another, was quite beyond him.

Make that two

Jack met Sophia off the plane, her hair a dark version of Shirley's. The wind whipped stray hair from the margins, which she deftly tucked back with bright-pink nails. Teenagers, eh? Got to love them. He delivered the negative news about her exams when they reached Petone. "I'm sorry, Dad," she said, sinking down in the passenger seat.

"It's a shame that your mother's been proved right," he said. "Let's just hope we hear better news from the Polytech."

"Me too."

"Now, let's hear about your holiday." Then he'd tell her about their visitor and Kathleen's passionate feelings about nail polish.

Goodness me

Jack was pleased at the way his girls accepted their roommate, and the spare mattress now stuck between their beds. Shirley proved irrepressible in the way she entertained his girls with her tales. Though when he heard laughter echo from their room he hoped the stories weren't too lurid. The girl's stay proved an advantage which was surprising; the way she mucked in to help Kathleen, throwing her weight behind the flower-planting, thinking it a lark. Even Sophia was coaxed outside when she heard her mother tell Shirley to select which ones to plant. "Not bad," Kathleen said, to the pansies and zinnias, "but I'll put the Livingstone daisies in a different bed."

Jack agreed to the girl staying longer, after Moira let them know Shirley's job application had fallen through. "If you get hold of the Hawke's Bay Herald," Kathleen said, "I'll make sure she looks for work."

It certainly was interesting watching the way Kathleen helped the girl. Calm; considerate. Why couldn't she form the same maternal alliance with her own children? The distinction saddened him.

There was a dance at the Silverstream Hall the day before Shirley's leaving, and Kathleen and Jack agreed to let the teens attend on the premise that Colin would keep an eye on the others. "I'll be on the stage with the band," he said. "Bird's eye view from there."

"What's say we go to the movies; forget them for a bit?"

"I'm not sure Jack."

"Well, I am. Time you got yourself gussied up."

*

"We'll drop you off, and meet you after the movies kids. Your mother wants to see *The Birds*."

"Do you really, Mum? It's supposed to be scary."

"All I said was, that I'd go with him. See you before eleven."

They were a few minutes late getting to the hall, and found Sophia and Bev sitting on a bench inside. James was on the floor, twisting to a Chubby Checker number, but not a sign of Shirley, and that was counting the bathroom.

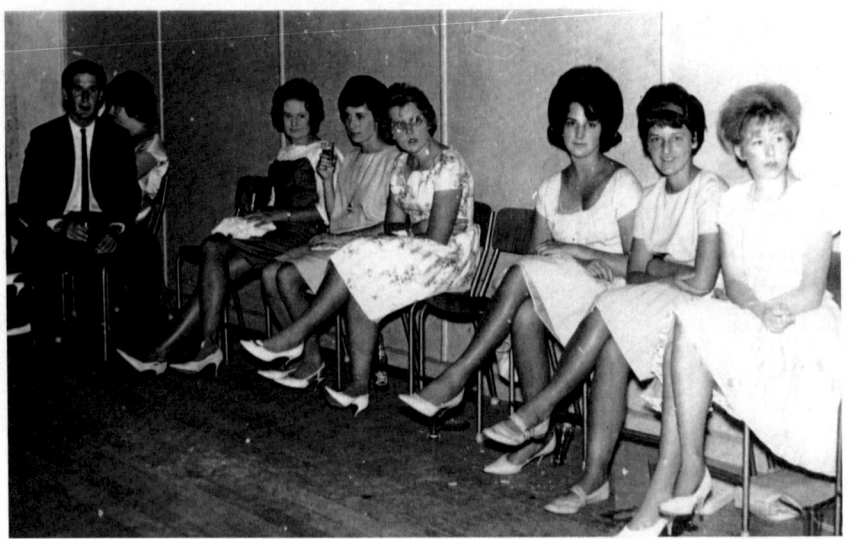
James and girls at dance.

"She said she felt sick and went home," Sophia said.

"Oh, God," Kathleen said. "C'mon, we're leaving."

The lights flicked on as they pulled up to the house which made Kathleen immediately suspicious, but Shirley came to the door, dressed in her housecoat and apologised for being a nuisance. "I've got a bad headache," she said. Her face was certainly flushed.

Kingi started barking and Jack went to check on him. A wandering cat, or hedgehog he thought, dragging the dog to his sleeping mat and calming him down.

It was after Shirley had been dispatched on the railcar, that they learned a local lad was seen late Saturday, sprinting down Terminus Street and across the footbridge. Heading to the hall, the new next-door neighbours had reported.

"Poor Moira and Tommy," Kathleen sighed.

"Might happen to us."

"Not if I have anything to do with it."

"I'm just saying…"

"Shut up, Jack."

"Loved the film though, didn't you?"

"Caw, caw."

New enterprises artistic and otherwise

Jack delivered Sophia to the Polytech the first day and boy did he feel proud. She was dressed in a white shift, a gold medallion around her neck and matching coloured jandals on her feet. The hair? Definitely aiming for a Mary Quant bob.

He introduced Sophia to James Coe, leaving him to show his daughter around. "Sophia can use our materials today," he said, "seeing she was given such short notice." Mr Coe turned to her. "You'll be doing a General Drawing class first thing." And as Jack watched them walk towards the room, he wished he could have joined her. Going to art school that would have been something; still, not complaining Jackie boy.

He popped into Websters art shop on Manners Street and purchased the supplies from the list Coe had given him, and grabbed some oil pastels and paper for himself, for his own art practice, when he found the time. But there was a money-making scheme he'd been thinking of for a while, which may just have to take precedence. Sophia would need a lift tomorrow, but then she would be making her own way to Wallace Street, taking the train and tram – he knew that she'd cope with that – taking to the school was the tricky matter.

Well, at least Sophia showed interest in the drawing classes and they soon became her favourite. She brought her drawings home to show around, and had just spread her sketches across the table one night when Jack lurched in clutching a bulging carton. "Sorry love," he said, motioning for her to clear a space, off-loaded the carton and shouted for James. "Come and give us a hand, I need help bringing in stuff from the car." Kathleen crossed to the table, lifted a cardboard flap and noted the stack of small glass jars and lids inside. Well, well. Just when she had thought the pickling at home idea was another of Jack's hair-brained schemes. And here Jack and James were now; humping in sacks of pearl onions and vinegar bottles through to the lean-to. She shook her head. Returned to chopping the carrots.

"Don't worry, they'll be kept out the back," he told her, entering the kitchen wiping sweat from his head, "but I will be ducking and diving in and out of the kitchen when it comes to filling the jars." Jack had burbled on about how easy it was to do your own pickling, as he'd seen the processes at the factory often enough. "I'll just make enough to sell locally, Kathleen. Should be fun."

"I hope you're listening carefully Jack. I am not peeling a single one."

"Did I ask you to?" That was his job. And maybe Dave's, as he was short of a job. As it was, he roped in whoever happened to be home at the time, including his art-student daughter and the other children's friends. He sterilised the jars in the old copper setting them out on a make-shift bench, carrying each batch of onions into the kitchen to heat in the largest jam pan Kathleen had ever seen. Said he'd bought it off Mr Narayan, whose wife found it too large for making chutney. She had a sudden vision of the poor woman, knees buckling under its weight, for even Jack struggled with lifting the pan from the stove.

The onions didn't produce the odour she had imagined, as Jack systematically completed each batch, although his nail brush got a good thrashing, with the staining from the skins.

Jack had designed his own labels and stacked them in piles around the kitchen table, small pots of paste and brushes too. Kathleen made herself scarce when the assembly line started groaning. "You've only got to paste them on," he told his kids. "I'm not asking you to eat the bloody onions."

"They taste good though, Dad."

"Thanks, Colin."

"I'm rather hoping others are going to love Crispa Onions too."

Not out of the woods yet

Just as life was lessened of some of its frustrations Jack was told by his doctor that he had adult-onset diabetes.

"I have to alter my diet, and get more exercise he said."

"Nothing new there."

Jack shrugged that one off. "He also suggested I might change my job."

"That's diabolical."

"Hang on. Hang on. I told him I drove for a living." What he didn't tell his wife, was that he had also been thinking along those lines, as his sacroiliac continued to bug him. The sitting didn't help his indigestion either. Not that he was too troubled about finding more work; novelty suited him.

That Saturday they went dancing, specifically so Jack could bend Bernie's ear, although he'd humoured Kathleen by saying it was for his health. Bernie had a milk run in the Hutt, and knew a lot of people – he might have heard about a job vacancy or two.

"Try Burns Philp," he suggested, "they're always looking for people."

"Right up my alley really, seeing I've experience with foodstuffs."

"We love those onions you gave us, by the way."

Yes, well. The onions. That was one enterprise where he hadn't got the work vs profits ratio right, as Kathleen had found it necessary to remind him. But he had found it fun. "Best join the ladies," he said, who were laying out food on the supper table. Jack eyed up the sausage rolls and felt his wife eyeing him, so stretched out a hand and picked up a curried egg.

*

Jack scored an interview for the Purchasing Officer's job, and within a week had handed in his notice to Murdoch's. "Maybe the doctor was wiser than I thought," Kathleen said. For Jack had also handed in the Austin A40. Yes, sometimes he had to admit, being forced into a decision was better than waiting for your own to strike. Now he would have a ten-minute walk to the station, then another from the train to his work. Repeated; it would be around an hour of compulsory daily exercise. He'd probably be too stuffed to play tennis.

Another car, another discovery

It was James who suggested his father should get another car as he wanted driving lessons. Get that, would you? Never figured him for a driving sort. The argument was, "most of my friends drive one." But of course, Jack got it. He needed a car to take girls out. Then blow me down, he changed his mind and Sophia said she'd like driving lessons. Give it a couple weeks, and he'd find himself a car, even if it meant dipping into his savings.

*

"She's had just the one owner," Reg Sykes said about the green Hillman Hunter. Sure, it has, Jack thought, probably turned the mileage back. But it ran well enough, and that had to count for something.

"I was hoping you'd get something like the old V8," Colin said.

"And I was rather hoping you'd be my mechanic."

"There's this Triumph Thunderbird I'm going to get."

"Another do-upper?"

"Not this one; she's in grouse condition."

"That'll make your mother happy."

"It will?"

"No more motorbike bits under your bed."

*

Whiteman's Valley, which lay off the end of Blue Mountains Road, was where Jack took Sophia driving. Farms and cabbage trees were the main landscape, plus a gentle winding dirt road. It would give him the opportunity to talk to her about the phone call they'd received from James Coe.

And to think Kathleen and he actually believed Sophia's

promises to redeem herself since that recent disastrous escapade. The night that she'd stuffed pillows in her bed and sneaked out the back door, and taken herself off to a party in Wellington. Kathleen's ire was breath-taking. She'd wanted to call the police the minute the empty bed was discovered; but held off until Jack had left the house. He found Sophia at Wellington railway station having missed the last train. He was bloody angry and felt like thumping her, but seeing her sitting with a cardigan pulled tight around her, softened him. It was jolly cold. He adjusted his hat, lit a smoke, sat beside her and listened to her explain why she'd done what she did, in the face of Kathleen's emphatic 'No' to her going out. "I just wanted to be with my art school friends Dad," she said, "And we just sat around sketching, that's all." Jack sighed, recalling young Shirley and her sneaking out antics, not so many months before. Clearly his daughter had gained a few tips in that department. He patted Sophia on the knee. "Just don't expect a grand reception," he said. And, because Kathleen had called the cops, they'd had to endure the questioning of Sophia in the wee hours, with his daughter trying to give her version of events to the policeman while Kathleen loudly interrupted and Jack tried his best to stay sane. And now this, he thought.

Sophia took to synchronising the clutch and pedals well, after just a few suggestions from him. "It makes sense to slow on the corners," she said. "I mean, I've travelled with you often enough to know that."

Why couldn't she be this savvy when it came to school? Coe had told him Sophia wasn't keeping up in the tests and had skipped some art classes too. Irate was the word to describe Kathleen's response. Leaping up so fast from the table she broke a cup, one with the nice red roses. "But he has said, my dear, that she has potential and would have her back."

"Some potential."

"She was too young, I guess."

"Immature more like it."

He took over driving at the junction where the road fed out. "I like driving," she said. "I wasn't even afraid of passing back there." Though, avoiding a man on a tractor was hardly a major hazard. Unless you counted the smell of straw and animal dung. He lit a cigarette, blowing the smoke out the window.

"Is this where you brought me in the truck, Dad, when I was little?"

"Yes, it is. I used to drive through Upper Hutt, because of the sealed road, and turn off from there."

"And you got me to write on the board..."

"And we sang?"

"*Doggie in the window.*"

"You have a terrific memory."

He pulled over on Main Street and parked. He really was a gutless wonder sometimes; it might be easier if he talked over tea. "Milkshake for you?"

Choosing a booth near the back, he sidled to the far side of the seat. "Mr Coe has been in touch," he said. That was enough for Sophia to open up about how she was never allowed to have boyfriends, or girlfriends either, and her mother didn't approve of...basically anything she did. He let her go on for a while, then interjected.

"And skipping class will change her thinking? Making us worry about who you're with and what you're doing?"

She shook her head.

"I have a suggestion for you to consider." This is so like last year he thought, instantly drained of energy. Sophia sucked on her straw. "That I look for a job for you that involves art?" She squinted when she looked up; more interested than upset. He could almost hear her brain ticking over. A job. Art. Money. "Please don't thank me – I've still got to run this past your mother."

New endeavours

Kathleen had thought Jack's plan 'brilliant.' If employed, Sophia would be forced to knuckle down, have to dress smartly. Pay board? Yes. A job was a very good suggestion indeed.

Jack hoped he wouldn't come across as an over-vigilant parent when visiting an advertising agency to enquire about the position for Junior Artist. But no, the boss was charming. Most understanding. "I have children," he said, lighting a pipe, relaxing in his chair. "Have her come and show us her portfolio," he said. "No promises though."

"They loved my ability to draw people," she told her parents, who had waited in their car outside, "and that they'd let me know soon." And, with Jack's urging, Kathleen stayed out of her way during that time, to avoid rocking their daughter's, and their own, equilibrium.

Two weeks down the line, and she was working in the Dixon Street art studio. And to Jack and Kathleen's relief, working hard; never letting on they had checked with her boss early on in the piece. Kathleen was certainly pleased to hear that the studio was impressed with her daughter.

James was also starting out on his own, and was at Teacher's College in Karori; spurred into that direction by his mother. "It will be nice to have another teacher in the family," she said. "Better than going to the seminary like some of his friends." That left Beverly the only one at high school, in the Fifth Form now, and still going well. No going off the rails that they had perceived, preferring to socialise locally with her church friends and sports' buddies. This year she'd taken up cricket and it hadn't escaped Jack's notice that she was shaping up well; quite the multi-disciplined girl.

*

Jack was enjoying the more relaxed environment around home. He was painting, trying out watercolours again, but just as he got the hang of the roses he'd been copying, he was introduced to a new interest. Plays. Theatre. Not going to shows but being part of them, since meeting work-mate Don who belonged to a drama club.

On a Tuesday night Don Finch picked him up off the bus at Stokes Valley, and took him to the hall where they practised. Oh yes, Jack was in his element. Reading plays and performing small parts, just for fun, with a group of like-minded people. He'd only been going there a short while when he fancied his hand at writing one; scribbling late into the night, exuberant about the script he was creating. James, who had met a girl at training college and often arrived home late, was the perfect audience for his father. Bursting forth with his latest lines to the bored listener was no deterrent for a man fired with enthusiasm. "Do you like the bit when he's accidentally run over a dog? I think I've got the right amount of pathos."

"Perfect, Dad. But please, I have to get up in a few hours."

*

When Jack met Brian Parker, who made models for sets at the club, he immediately thought of Sophia. She was enjoying her job, and mixing with the other youngsters through the day, but every night she was home with the family. "I think I'll take her with me," he told Kathleen, "and my watercolours; she'd be a good help with the model sets."

Photoshoot for play.

Jack auditioned for a part of an army sergeant in a play with the stupidest title Kathleen, had ever heard: *The Amorous Prawn.* For goodness sakes. Jack didn't care what it was called as long as he got on the stage. But they were missing an actress for a very small part. "Dad, I can't act," Sophia protested, when he suggested she take it on. "All you have to do," he said, flicking through the script, "is to look adoringly at some chap. Shouldn't be too hard. Should it?" The worst part she discovered, was learning the play was being performed in a local hall and that her father had asked half the world along.

*

Jack decided he was more artist than actor, which met with approval from his family, returning to the Hutt River to paint in oils, and attending the occasional art class at Wellington art school. Thanks to Sophia, who met tutor John Drawbridge in the street, and he asked what she was doing. "You should come to the night class we run," he said, "It would be a shame to lose that talent."

Naturally Jack would take the car those nights, and both of them would compare notes on the drive home; about the class, and the boyfriend – a trainee policeman. Kathleen thought this a suitable vocation it seemed, and tolerated him arriving in his blue Morris Minor and taking Sophia for drives on a Sunday.

Kathleen often played piano when the house was quiet, although she was a little rusty; the notes she'd once run over smoothly she sometimes missed, and would have to start again. Jack would recall earlier days when she'd sat absorbed in the music and he would attend to some little thing in the room so he could listen. Or sing along. Yep, couldn't live with her; couldn't live without her. He waited until her hands rested on the keys. "How about we go to the movies tonight?"

She turned in the seat. "What's on?"

"*Strange Bedfellows.*"

"That's the one with Rock Hudson, isn't it?"

"And Gina Lollobrigida."

*

Kathleen and Jack saw little of the boys as the months drifted on. They were out most evenings; Colin with his music-making friends and James with his girlfriend Jenny. She had her own little car, and 'a good head on her shoulders' as Kathleen had described her, a perfect foil for James who, like his father, loved spinning yarns as if they were the latest fashion. Jack still sang silly songs with James if he got the chance and regaled him or Jenny about his latest enterprises.

When they returned home from a dance one night, they found Jack with a long cardboard roll in his hand, formerly a lunch-wrap inner, which he lifted to his eye like Napoleon and viewed the image tacked on the wall from several feet down the passage. "To check the perspective, and nuances of tone," he informed, as he took them through the paces. Whether or not his drawings or paintings improved from this viewing, no-one was going to tell him. To James, when he was told to close one eye at a time, could see little that night. He later learned from an optician, that it wasn't his father's impressionistic style that ruined his sight, but the lack of 20/20 vison.

Then, to Jack's delight, he was awarded a prize at the Hutt Valley Arts exhibition, with the very same painting – a view to the hills from the river. The family read and re-read the type on the card which described Jack McPhee as 'up and coming'. And although Kathleen preferred realism, she came to admire this work, with the brushstrokes showing in the thickly applied paint, and the trees she'd described as daubs.

Soon after, a chap called Pat asked him to help clean the Woolworths building in the evenings. "Just part-time, Jack – bit of pocket money." He might have got a few pounds for his labours, and found the odd thing in bins he could use, but by Christmas he'd had a guts-full of cleaning other people's muck and said adios to the job – and acquaintance.

1966

By March, Jack was feeling increasingly tired and out of breath. He took himself to a doctor near his work and after giving Jack the once over he wrote on two sheets of paper. "That indigestion you've described just might be angina," he said, and handed him a prescription. "Pills to alleviate the discomfort, and this is a form for you to fill in, as you need further tests at the hospital."

Jack kept the news to himself for a while, awaiting the 'right' moment to impart it. Unfortunately, it was Sophia who learned prematurely of his worsening health, when he fainted outside the drawing class one Thursday evening. A tutor helped him to the students' common room, and then fetched his daughter. He was propped against pillows, a pill in one hand, a glass of water in another, oblivious to his haggard appearance. "Dad,' she said. "What happened?" He tried to wave her anxiety aside, by telling her he was much better, thank you, and that she should finish the class.

She went back, just to pack up and give her apologies to her tutor. Mr Drawbridge went with her to check on Jack. "Sorry to have mucked up your class, John, but I'll be right in a jiffy."

"Are you sure? I can drive you home, if you like." And before her father could answer, Sophia said, "Thank you, Mr Drawbridge, but I can take him."

"There are two things I want you to keep from your mother," Jack told her on the way, "one, is about what happened tonight, as I need to tell her. And, the other is, that you weren't driving the car."

*

What Jack never learned was the burden of that promise. On a Saturday night in early June, when they had just finished dinner, Jack said he felt a bit crook and moved to sit in an armchair in the lounge. "How about a bit of Sid James?" he said to Colin, and the television was turned on. Kathleen saw Jack slump in the chair and rushed over. "Phone the doctor Colin. Right now. Now!" she screeched, and waved the girls away.

Colin hung up the phone. "He's coming right away."

"Now Colin," Kathleen said, taking a deep breath and speaking concisely, "Take the girls next door and come back *immediately.*"

*

Sophia remembers it being late when she and Beverly were escorted home by the neighbours, the sky dark. The air freezing. Inside, their mother and brothers were lined up like statues beside the piano. "Your father isn't here," Kathleen said, her voice shaking.

"Has he gone to hospital?"

Kathleen shook her head. "No. Not the hospital."

"Where *is* Dad?" "Where *is* he?"

"He ... he's been taken to the mortuary." She paused for a moment, held her hands out to the girls. "He said he was sorry that he couldn't say goodbye."

*

Following a funeral service at St. Mary's church, Silverstream, Jack McPhee's body was taken to Akatawara cemetery for burial. His wife Kathleen was buried beside him forty-five years later.